Patchwork Complete Beginners

Kirstye .Q Atkinsonb

How patchwork, a traditional craft, can enhance your life

The majority of us are familiar with patchwork, whether it be from a grandmother's handcrafted quilted bedspread or a trendy jacket we purchased on Etsy. Patchwork, which entails sewing several pieces of fabric together to create a larger design, is most frequently used to create quilts, but it is also used to create tablecloths, cushion covers, tapestries, and clothing, among other things. Landscapes or asymmetrical patterns can be incorporated into the overall design, as well as abstract geometrical patterns on hexagonal or rectangular grids, for instance.

Patchwork is frequently used as a frugal method of utilizing leftover fabric, but it has also come to mean artistic expression, producing works that frequently become family heirlooms. It's a method that has been used for countless years and is used all over the world.

The tradition of hand sewing patchwork quilts and other similar items was severely harmed by the industrialization of textile production, but the craft has recently experienced something of a renaissance.

All the Basics

This is a step-by-step guide to making a quilt, from gathering supplies and choosing fabrics to basic quilt construction. Although I know it's easier said than done, I recommend choosing a first project that doesn't have a deadline attached to it (such as a baby shower or birthday) and working at your own pace to complete each step, one at a time. You can do this!

If you've quilted before, I hope you can still find one or two helpful tips in this section.

Materials and Supplies

When shopping for supplies, a good rule of thumb is to buy the best-quality materials you can afford. You'll be spending a lot of time making and using your quilt, so invest in materials that you'll be happy with for the long term.

Materials

You probably already know that you need fabric, thread, and batting. This section talks about them in a little more detail.

Fabric

Finding new fabrics to use is one of my favorite parts of quiltmaking! The variety of fabrics available to today's quilters is truly amazing. Solid fabrics are available in hundreds of colors, and each new wave of print fabrics seems more fabulous than the last.

Almost all print fabric made for quilting is 100% cotton. Cotton is easy to work with, washable, and durable. It's a good choice for quilters, and its long life means you'll be enjoying your quilt for years to come.

Most cotton quilting fabrics are of a similar, medium weight, but other types, such as chambray, twill, poplin, and double gauze, are all suitable for quiltmaking.

Fabric that is 100% linen lends a natural look and a lot of texture. It can be an excellent choice for setting off bright colors or complementing muted ones. Linen can be tricky to work with, as its looser weave is prone to raveling, but the unique look of natural linen can be worth the extra work.

Linen/cotton blends are my favorite solid fabrics. The blend offers some of the weight and texture of linen, but with the stability and tighter weave of cotton. Because it provides a nice contrast in texture to the smoother blocks, I like to use linen/cotton blends for sashing.

SAMPLE FABRICS

1. Double gauze

2. Cotton print

3. Twill

4. Poplin

5. Linen

6. Linen/cotton blend

7. Selvage

Don't hesitate to include unconventional fabrics, such as madras plaids, vintage bed linens, and shirting cottons, in your compositions. Just keep in mind that the projects in this book (and patchwork quilting projects in general) will be most successful when constructed of stable woven fabrics that can be washed and ironed.

Remember also that delicate fabrics wear more quickly and may not be the best choice for a quilt that will get heavy use over many years.

Note: For more about prints and how to choose the right ones for your quilt, see <u>page 24</u>.

FABRIC VOCABULARY

The project instructions will make more sense if you familiarize yourself with the following terms.

SELVAGE is the finished edge of the fabric. The selvages of quilting fabrics are usually printed with the name of the fabric and designer and are often quite attractive by themselves. Some quilters like to save their selvages to use in other projects (see the photo on <u>page 7</u>).

FOLD refers to the center fold created when fabric is folded selvage to selvage, as it is on the bolt.

GRAIN refers to the way the threads in the weave of a woven fabric line up with the selvage. With cotton and linen fabrics, the grain is parallel and perpendicular to the selvage. Fabric cut along the grain is stable and ideal for patchwork piecing.

tip

It can be difficult to identify the right and wrong sides of some fabrics, especially solids and batiks. In theory, you should choose one side and stick with it. In practice, it can be difficult to keep track of which side is which. Don't spend too much time fretting about the difference between seemingly identical right and wrong sides. If you can't tell the difference, it's unlikely to harm your project.

BIAS means diagonal in relation to the grain. Fabric cut on the bias (for instance, fabric that has been cut into triangles) has a tendency to stretch along the bias edge and requires careful handling.

WIDTH is the distance from selvage to selvage. In most cases this is about 42″–44″. (In order to account for a wide variety of fabrics, the projects in this book assume a 40″ width unless otherwise stated.)

LENGTH is the distance from cut edge to cut edge, along the selvage. The length of the fabric is the length of the cut. For instance, a perfect 2-yard cut should be 72″ in length.

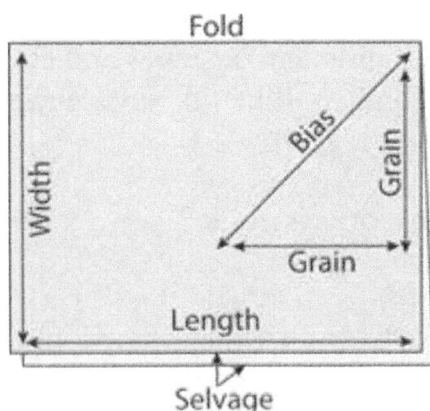

RIGHT AND WRONG SIDES The right side of the fabric is the side you want showing in your finished project—usually the side with a pattern printed on it. The wrong side is, of course, the opposite side, which you don't want to show.

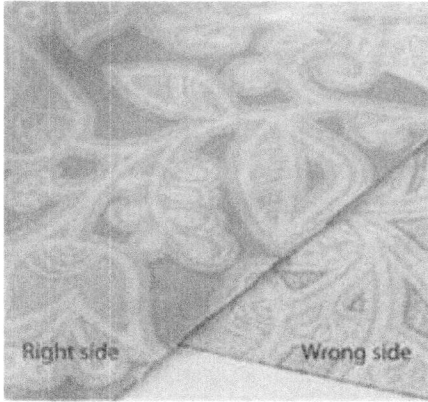

Right side · Wrong side

ELEMENTS OF A QUILT

A quilt is like a sandwich. It has a fabric top, a fabric back, and a layer of batting in the middle. The quilt top and back are usually made using patchwork, a technique in which smaller pieces of fabric are sewn together, often in blocks that have a repeating pattern. The layers of the quilt sandwich are held together by quilting, and the raw edges are finished with a binding.

COMMON FABRIC CUTS

Yardage

In the United States, cotton quilting fabric is sold by the yard and is usually 42″–44″ wide. Most quilt shops sell fabric in ⅛-yard (4½″) increments, with ⅛ yard being the minimum cut. Online retailers usually have a larger minimum cut, most often ¼ yard (9″) or ½ yard (18″).

tip

Buying fat-quarter bundles can be a quick way to get small pieces of a range of coordinating fabrics.

Fat quarters

A fat quarter is created by cutting a yard of fabric in half along both its length and width, creating a piece of fabric about 18″ × 21″–22″. These "fatter" ¼-yard pieces allow different cutting possibilities than the standard 9″ × width of fabric ¼-yard cuts.

11

Not all shops sell fat quarters cut from the bolt, but most sell precut fat quarters, either individually or in bundles of coordinating prints.

Standard ¼-yard cuts and fat quarters are not necessarily interchangeable, so always purchase the type of cut specified in the project instructions.

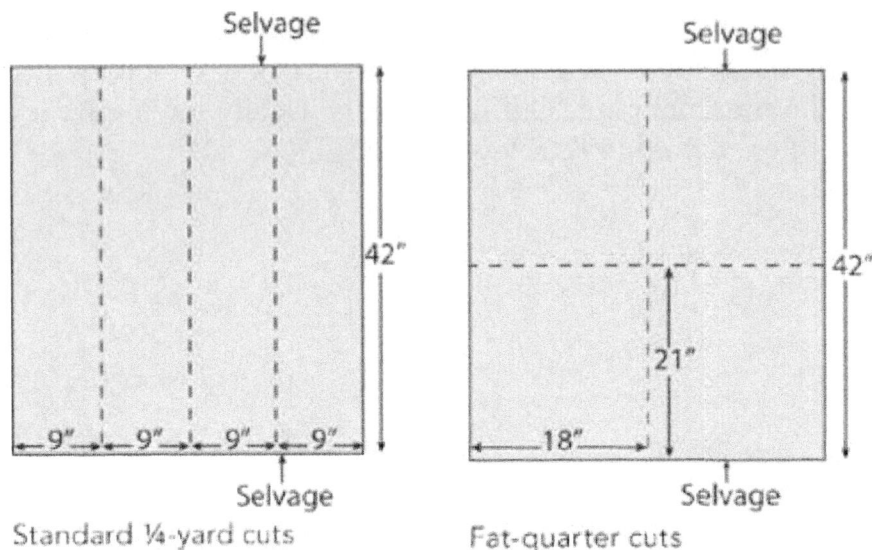

Standard ¼-yard cuts

Fat-quarter cuts

tip

Most manufacturers produce print fabrics in "collections" of coordinating prints. A collection will typically include coordinating small-, medium-, and large-scale prints in several different colors. Collections by well-known designers (often called "designer fabrics") are eagerly anticipated in the quilting world and are usually available for only a limited amount of time.

If you're having trouble choosing coordinating print fabrics, buying prints that all come from the same collection can be a great shortcut.

Precut squares

Some manufacturers sell packages of fabric squares cut to 5″ × 5″. These sets usually include one print each from a particular collection. Among the most popular are Moda's Charm Squares. (In fact, Moda's product is so popular that most people refer to 5″ squares generically as charms or charm squares!)

If you're cutting your own squares from cut fabric yardage, you can expect to get 8 squares from ¼ yard, 12 squares from a fat quarter, and 24 squares from ½ yard.

Precut strips

Some fabric manufacturers and quilt shops sell bundles of fabric strips precut to 2½″ × width of fabric. Different manufacturers have different names for these; some examples are Moda's Jelly Rolls, Robert Kaufman's Roll Ups, and Westminster's Designer Rolls.

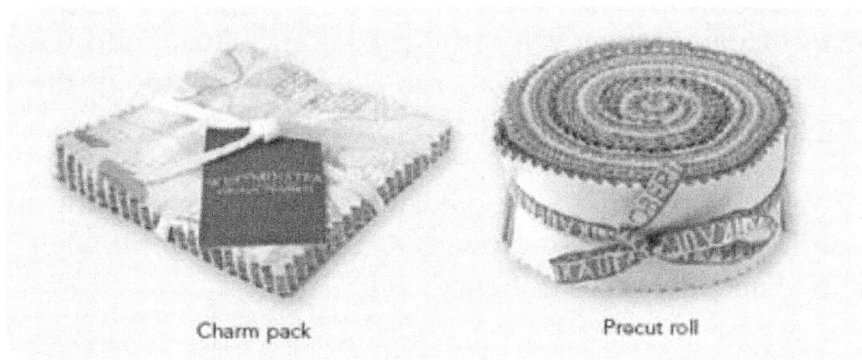

Charm pack   Precut roll

TO WASH OR NOT TO WASH?

Quilters tend to have strong opinions about whether or not to wash fabric before use. There are arguments for both sides.

tip

Precut fabrics such as precut squares and strips should not be prewashed!

PREWASHING:

- Removes any residual chemicals from the printing/dyeing process
- Helps prevent bleeding in your finished product
- Helps prevent uneven shrinkage in your finished product
- Is a good way to test a fabric's durability

NOT PREWASHING:

- Conserves resources
- Saves time
- Means that none of your fabric is lost due to raveling in the wash

If you're using only high-quality fabrics designed for quilting, the likelihood of bleeding or uneven shrinkage is fairly low. Unfortunately, you just won't know for sure until you run your fabric through the wash, so prewashing is generally the safest course of action.

If you prewash your fabrics, use cold water and your washing machine's gentlest setting. Tumble dry on low, but remove the fabric when it is still very slightly damp and press it immediately.

tip

Don't let your desire for "the crinkly look" (see page 12) affect your decision as to whether or not to prewash your fabric. Using natural-fiber batting is what really creates that texture!

Batting

Low-loft cotton batting is the choice of most contemporary quilters. All the quilts in this book were made with low-loft cotton batting. Cotton batting clings to fabric, making sandwiching and quilting easier. It makes a flat, warm quilt that gets softer each time it's washed.

tip

If you want to make a lighter-weight quilt, consider replacing the batting layer with preshrunk cotton flannel. Piece the flannel as you would a quilt top or back (see pages 20 and 29), press the seams open, and sandwich and quilt the project just as you would with batting. The finished quilt will be lighter but will crinkle just as it would with batting.

THE CRINKLY LOOK

Another characteristic of cotton batting is the crinkly texture it creates after washing.

Many in the modern quilting community have embraced "the crinkly look." This refers to the old-fashioned-looking texture created after a quilt is washed and dried. The texture is caused by natural-fiber batting shrinking and shifting inside the quilt sandwich.

The crinkles make for a softer quilt, but they can also obscure some detail in piecing and print fabrics.

If you want to avoid a crinkly-looking quilt, you may want to use polyester or a polyester/cotton blend batting instead.

Before washing

After washing

HOW DO I GET BATTING THE RIGHT SIZE FOR MY QUILT?

Batting is sold in prepackaged pieces (usually corresponding to bedding sizes, explained on page 18) or by the yard from giant rolls.

tip

If you plan to preshrink natural-fiber batting, be sure to buy enough to account for the shrinkage.

PACKAGED BATTING Even if you're working with supposedly standard bedding sizes, you're unlikely to find packaged batting in exactly the size you're looking for. Look instead for a piece that is large enough that you could theoretically cut the size you need from it. For instance, if you need an 80″ × 80″ piece of batting, you could use a 90″ × 96″ packaged batting, but a 72″ × 90″ piece would be too small.

BATTING BY THE YARD When buying batting by the yard, start by checking the width of the batting on the roll. Make sure it's wide enough to cut the piece you need. For instance, if you need a 100″ × 100″ piece of batting, a roll that's only 90″ wide won't work.

Once you find a roll that's wide enough, purchase enough yardage to cut out the size you need. For instance, if you need an 80″ × 80″ piece of batting, a 2¼-yard (81″) cut from a 90″-wide roll of batting should work.

As long as the batting is the same size or larger than the dimensions required for your project, don't waste time cutting it down to the exact recommended size until you make the quilt sandwich (see page 32). At that point, you can lay the batting and quilt top out on the floor and use the quilt top as a guide to cut the batting to the correct size.

Recommended batting sizes in this book are 4″ larger than the finished quilt tops.

Thread

For piecing and quilting, use only high-quality 100% cotton or 100% polyester thread. Using cheap bargain-bin thread will make getting a good stitch difficult, if not impossible.

I recommend choosing a neutral color of thread for piecing and quilting (using thread the same color as the solid sashing is often a good choice) and using the same thread in the bobbin.

If you buy thread specifically designed for quilting, make sure it's machine quilting thread. Hand quilting thread has a waxy coating and shouldn't be used in your sewing machine.

Supplies

You need only a few basic tools and supplies to make any quilt in this book. Here are my recommendations. Basic quilting supplies are usually available at both local quilt shops and larger craft supply stores.

Rotary cutter

Choose a 45mm or 60mm rotary cutter that fits comfortably in your hand. Your rotary cutter is the quilting equivalent of dressmaker's shears, so you'll want to get something sturdy that you'll be comfortable using for years to come. Replace dull blades with new ones in the correct size and from the same manufacturer. I find that my rotary cutter blades usually last through two to three projects before I have to replace them.

Self-healing cutting mat

Choose a mat with easily readable numbers and 1″ grid lines. I recommend a mat that's at least 24″ × 36″. If that's not realistic, choose a mat that's at least 18″ × 24″. The larger your mat, the less you'll need to readjust fabric while you're cutting, so a large mat will both save time and encourage accuracy.

Rulers

Clear plastic quilting rulers come in a vast array of shapes and sizes. The two essentials are a 6″ × 24″ long rectangle and a 12½″ square. Both should have ¼″ grid lines. The 12½″ square should have a diagonal (45° angle) line running from corner to corner. I also get a lot of use out of my 4″ × 14″ ruler, as I find it less cumbersome for cutting smaller pieces.

Iron and ironing board

The iron and ironing board you already have are probably fine. Just make sure that both the iron and ironing board cover are clean. I recommend pressing with the steam setting on. However, if your iron is prone to spitting up rusty water, you may want to use it dry with a spray bottle.

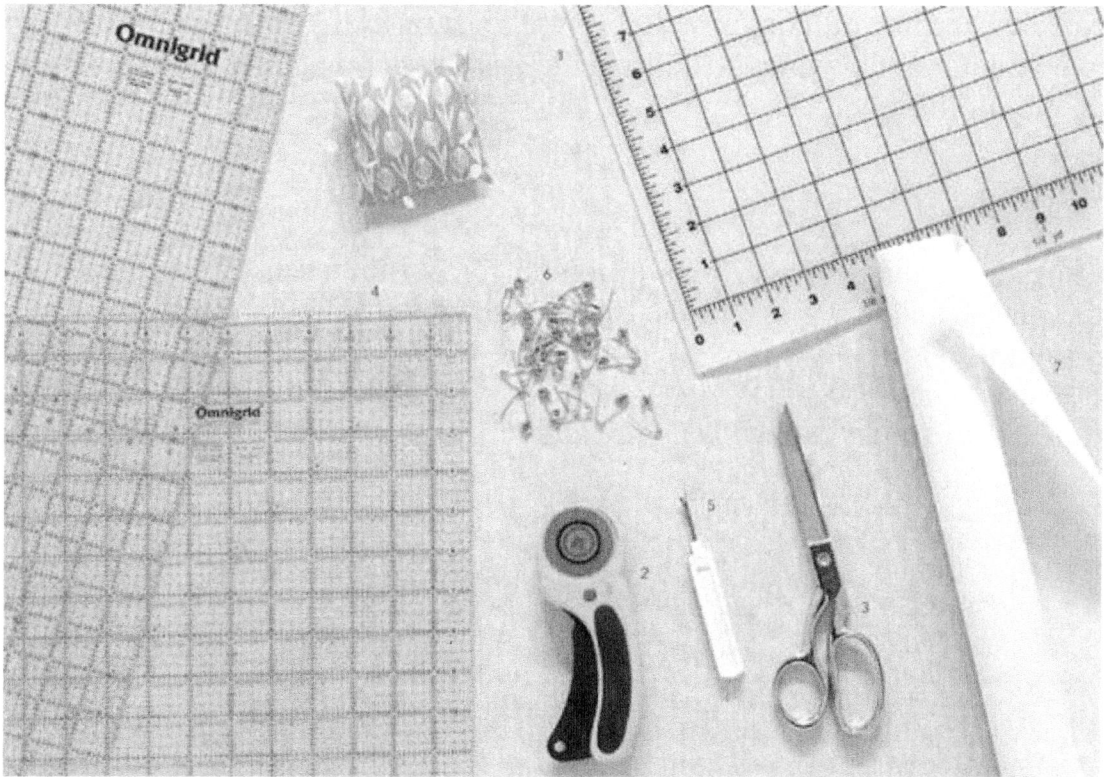

1. Cutting mat 2. Rotary cutter 3. Scissors 4. Rulers 5. Seam ripper 6. Pins 7. Fusible web

Machine sewing needles

Needles come in a variety of sizes and types. For patchwork piecing, choose mid-size (70/10–80/12) needles based on the kind of fabric you're using. For quilting cotton and linen fabrics, universal needles are usually fine. If you're using a finer fabric like double gauze or a tighter weave like poplin, Microtex/sharp needles are more appropriate. Microtex/sharp needles are also a good choice for machine appliqué. For machine quilting, choose heavier (90/14) machine quilting needles. If your needles are breaking often during quilting, consider switching to a heavier needle.

Needles become dull quickly, so be sure to change them after every eight to twelve hours of sewing. A dull needle will have a negative impact on the quality of the stitch.

Straight pins

Choose the sharp, longer pins designed for quilting. I use pins with both flat plastic and tiny glass heads. Either one will work fine for the projects in this book.

Note: Discard any bent pins immediately!

Basket of scrap fabric

Scissors

Although most of your cutting will be done with a rotary cutter, you'll still want to have a pair of dedicated fabric scissors on hand. To keep them sharp, never use your fabric scissors on paper. This includes appliqués made with paper-backed fusible web (see below), which should be cut using everyday craft scissors.

Seam ripper

Sometimes you just have to take some stitches out and start over. A seam ripper makes this easy to do without damaging the fabric. Keep one in your work area at all times and never hesitate to use it.

Fabric-marking tools

I prefer disappearing ink or water-erasable ink fabric markers, as I find them easier to use for marking fabric. Tailor's chalk is another popular option, particularly for darker fabrics. Whatever you use, test it on scrap fabric first to confirm that it really can be removed.

Fusible web

Fusible web is basically a thin layer of iron-on adhesive used to hold two pieces of fabric together. Fusible web is sold in packages or by the yard and comes with a layer of waxy paper on one side or both sides of the adhesive. For the simple machine appliqué in this book, purchase fusible web with paper on only one side. I usually use HeatnBond Lite.

Pay attention to the difference between light and heavyweight (or "no-sew") fusible webbing. Only lightweight products are designed to be used with sewing machines.

Safety pins

Safety pins designed for quilting have a slightly curved shape. You'll need at least a hundred, and often several hundred, pins to pin baste a quilt sandwich (see page 32).

Tools for finishing binding

Use binding clips (often mistaken for barrettes) or straight pins to hold the binding in place and a sharp hand-sewing needle for hand finishing.

Painter's tape

This is the same blue tape available at home improvement and variety stores. Use it to secure the quilt back to the floor before adding the quilt top and batting, and during pin basting. Because it doesn't damage interior surfaces such as hard floors, it's an invaluable aid in making a quilt sandwich.

Organizer cards and labels

This is my generic term for pieces of cardstock or other heavy paper used to keep quilt blocks organized during piecing. You can buy a package of letter-sized cardstock or simply round up stray pieces of pasteboard from around the house. Cereal box panels, Priority Mail envelopes, and pieces of paper shopping bags all make great organizer cards. I use them as dividers, to stack the fabrics belonging to each block so they won't get all mixed up. Garage sale labels and sticky notes are also useful for tagging blocks and cut pieces during construction.

Plastic tubs and baskets

Chances are you won't finish your quilt in one day, so you'll need somewhere to put all that cut fabric. Clear plastic tubs with lids are great for keeping fabric and unfinished projects organized.

Unless you plan to throw them all away (which would be a shame!), you'll also want to keep a basket or bin around to collect scraps. It may not seem like much at first, but as you work on more projects, your collection of scraps will grow and grow. Before you know it, you'll have enough to make entire projects just from your scraps.

Planning Your Quilt

Once you've chosen the quilt pattern you want to make, the fun of planning it begins. You'll need to decide what size you want your quilt to be and—best of all—what fabrics you want to use.

What size?

Quilts are incredibly versatile. You can make a quilt for any size bed, for a crib, to use as a throw, or to hang on the wall.

tip

Here are general guidelines for bed quilt sizes:

Twin: *65"–70" wide × 85"–90" long*
Full/Queen: *85"–95" wide × 85"–95" long*
King: *90"–95" wide × 105"–110" long*

Making quilts for beds

Bed quilt sizes are determined by calculating how much quilt will overhang the mattress on all sides. I'm not particularly fussy about having my bedding fall at a specific point. However, bed quilts are a big investment in time and fabric, so I think it's a good idea to measure your mattress, your current bedding, or both before you start planning your quilt—just so you can get a feel for what your finished quilt might look like on the bed.

Making lap quilts

Medium-sized quilts for relaxing at home or using as a picnic or beach blanket are often referred to as "lap quilts."

I like to make lap quilts at least as long as the height of the person who will be using them. (That usually means the quilt will be large enough for the recipient to cover his or her feet when relaxing on the sofa.)

Making quilts for babies

A conventional crib quilt is approximately $45'' \times 60''$, but a smaller quilt that can be taken along in a stroller or car seat is often a more practical baby gift. I like to make baby quilts that measure $30''$–$45''$ on each side.

Making quilts to hang on the wall

Mini quilts—or "doll quilts," as they're often called—can be a fun addition to your home décor. Mini quilts are often made from one or just a few blocks, so making a mini version of a project can be a good way to try out a piecing technique before committing to a larger quilt.

Make a mini quilt wall-ready by folding squares of fabric in half diagonally and sewing them to the top corners on the back of the quilt before you add the binding. Once the binding is finished, tuck a dowel or piece of balsa wood into the pockets to create a rigid hanger. *This method is best for small quilts that are 24" or less in width.*

Adjusting quilt sizes

Each pattern in this book includes the size of its finished quilt blocks. If you want to adjust the size of one of the quilt patterns, start with the size of the finished quilt blocks.

For patterns with no sashing between blocks:

This applies to *Snapshots* (page 51), *Small Plates* (page 56), *Valentine* (page 71), *Little Leaves* (page 88), *Sunspot* (page 96), and *Superstar* (page 104).

Simply calculate how many blocks you'll need to make a quilt in the desired size and make that many more or fewer blocks. Note that most of the patterns rely on a checkerboard or otherwise rotating block layout that may be affected by using a different number of blocks—especially if you switch from an even to an odd number of blocks in a row or column or vice versa.

For patterns with only exterior border sashing:

This applies to *Fenced In* (page 46), *Kitchen Window* (page 77), and Birdbath (page 112).

Use the same basic process as for quilts without sashing, but increase or decrease the length of the exterior border sashing to match the new quilt size. If you're making a significantly larger quilt, don't hesitate to piece the border sashing from several shorter pieces of fabric.

For patterns with sashing between blocks:

This applies to *Batch of Brownies* (page 62), *Planetarium* (page 82), and *Rain or Shine* (page 118).

Adjusting the size of these patterns will be a bit more complicated because you'll need to include the size of the sashing in your calculation. Drawing the planned layout on graph paper can be extremely helpful.

What about the back?

In most cases, changing the size of the quilt top will require significant modification to the quilt back described in the pattern. However, this book includes a variety of quilt back sizes and styles. Instead of reconfiguring a pattern's back design to a different size, consider browsing the other patterns for a layout that's already close to the size of the quilt you're making.

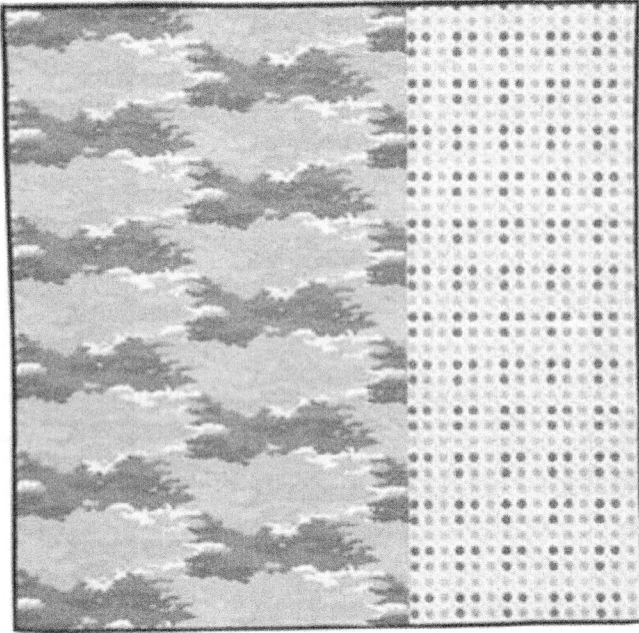

Back of *Batch of Brownies* (full quilt on page 62)

Back of *Kitchen Window* (full quilt on page 77)

Quilt backs are also a great place to experiment with freestyle piecing and to use scraps left over from making the quilt top.

Back of *Small Plates* (full quilt on page 56)

Choosing fabrics

The fabrics you choose are a big part of what will make your quilt special and uniquely yours!

All about color

The color wheel is a tool used to demonstrate color relationships. It's sort of like a circular rainbow and can be a helpful guide for choosing effective color schemes.

If you have a hard time making fabric choices, I suggest purchasing a color wheel tool from your local art supply or quilt shop. When you see a fabric or composition that you like, refer to your color wheel to determine which color schemes you respond to. The *3-in-1 Color Tool* (available from C&T Publishing) is a great choice.

While the following is in no way an exhaustive exploration of color theory, familiarizing yourself with the color concepts and color schemes presented here may make it easier to choose fabrics for your quilt.

WARM VS. COOL

Reds, oranges, and yellows are considered warm colors, while greens, blues, and violets are considered cool colors. In general, warm colors "advance," or appear more prominent in a composition, while cool colors "recede," or stay in the background.

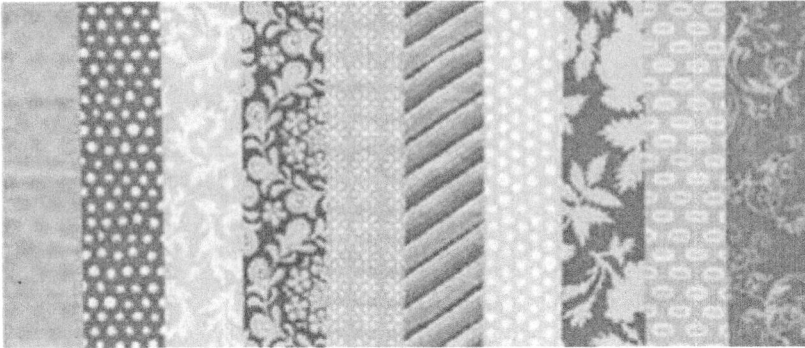

Warm colors

Cool colors

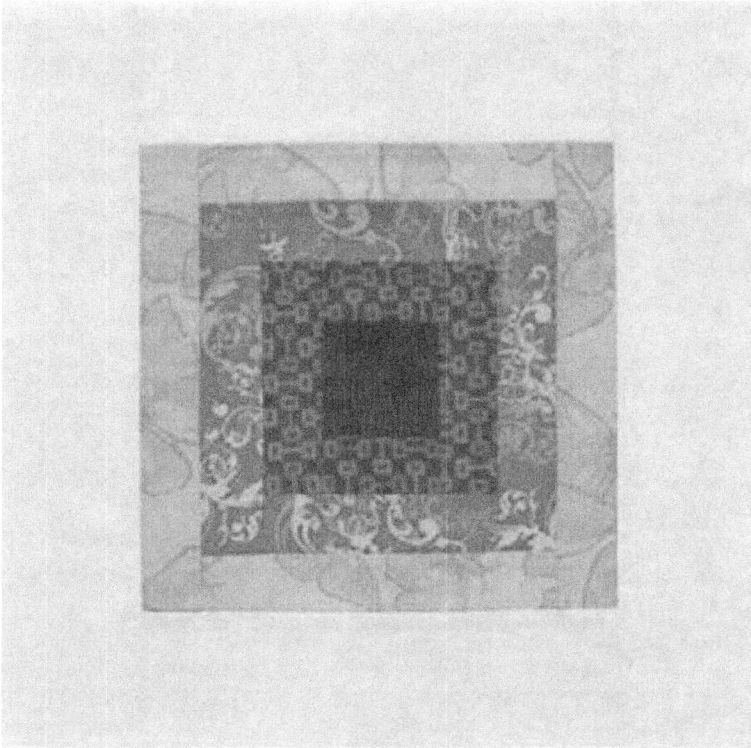

An example of value gradation from light to dark orange

A neutral composition using browns and grays

tip

Many of the patterns in this book call for a neutral solid fabric for sashing. White, gray, and natural linen are all good choices for neutral solids.

More- and less-intense yellow fabrics

VALUE

Value refers to the lightness or darkness of a color. For example, pink is a lighter value of red. In general, combining fabrics that have some contrast in value will make for a more interesting composition.

INTENSITY

Intensity is a way of describing the brightness or dullness of a color. For example, mustard yellow is less intense than canary. Colors of similar intensity tend to look most harmonious together, but pairing colors of differing intensity can provide an interesting contrast.

NEUTRALS

Grays and browns are considered neutral colors. Although they aren't truly colors, black and white can also be considered neutral. With neutral colors, it helps to pay attention to the temperature (i.e., whether the color is warm or cool). In general, grays and blacks are cooler than beiges and browns. Look closely, though. Sometimes you'll see a really warm rosy gray or sharp bluish brown.

A monochromatic composition using greens

A complementary color scheme using orange and blue

An analogous composition using red-violets, reds, oranges, and golds

MONOCHROMATIC COLOR SCHEME

A monochromatic color scheme is one that uses only one color. Combining fabrics of varying values and intensities of that color can make a monochromatic color scheme more interesting.

ANALOGOUS COLOR SCHEME

Analogous colors are grouped next to each other on the color wheel. Using an analogous color scheme is an easy way to use a lot of color harmoniously.

COMPLEMENTARY COLORS

Complementary colors are the colors across from one another on the color wheel. These "opposite" colors offer a lot of contrast and can create a striking color scheme.

So many prints!

I'm often asked for advice about how to choose print fabrics for a quilt, and my answer is always the same: Use what you like. It may seem overly simplistic, but I think relying on your own taste is really the best way to end up with a project that you're happy with.

If you're really uncomfortable with the idea of choosing a bunch of different fabrics, look instead for a fabric collection (page 10) you find appealing and buy all the fabric for your quilt from that same collection.

When shopping for fabrics, it's easy to be drawn in by the flamboyant large-scale florals or the adorably kitschy animal prints. Those louder prints have their place, but don't discount the importance of basics, such as dots, stripes, smaller florals, and other small- and medium-scale prints.

Large-scale prints

Medium-scale prints

Small-scale prints

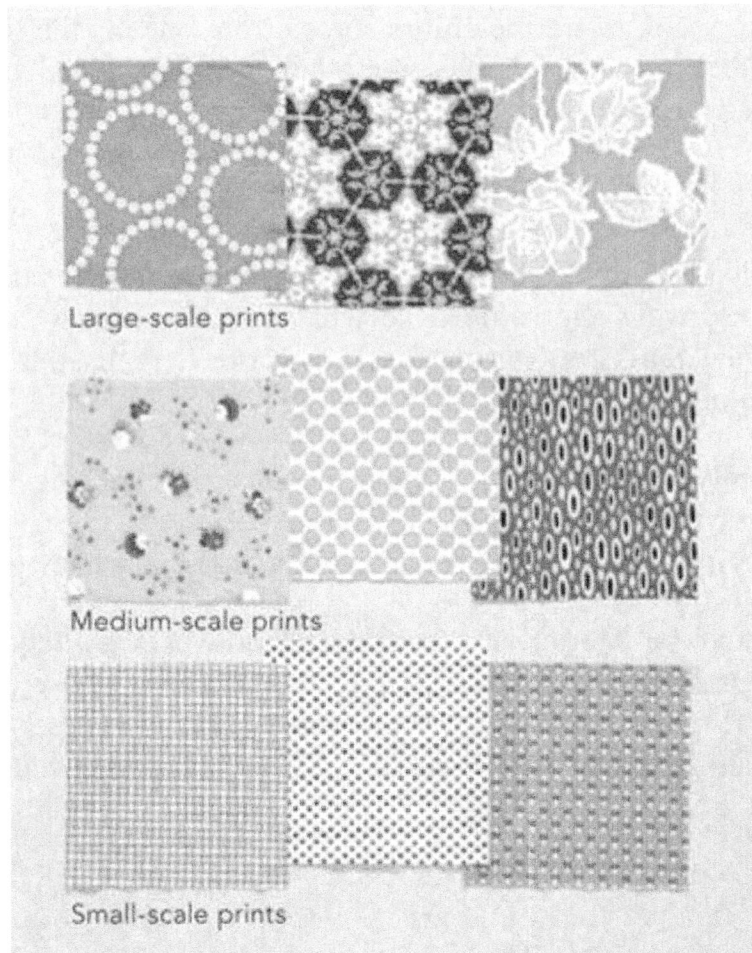

When choosing prints for patchwork, think about how they'll look when cut up. Does that small print have so much negative (empty) space that the actual print part won't show up on half the pieces? Is that large print so big that the pieces cut from it will look like they're from entirely different pieces of fabric? Decide whether you can make difficult prints work (for instance, by fussy cutting the parts you want, as described on page 28), or whether you want to move on to something different.

tip

Most print fabrics have a regular pattern that can be turned in any direction without appearing to be upside down. Prints that do have a definite top and bottom are called directional prints.

If you're using a directional print, you may want to sew pieces cut from it so that the placement of the "top" and "bottom" of the print is consistent throughout your quilt. That doesn't necessarily mean that the top and bottom of the print are oriented to the top and bottom of the quilt—just that the direction of the print is consistent throughout your composition.

Of course, these are just my opinions. One great thing about making quilts is that there are so many different ways to approach the same basic pattern. I really encourage you to trust your own personal taste and use the patterns in this book to create compositions that appeal to you personally.

Step-by-Step Quilt Construction

As with most things, there's more than one way to make a quilt. This chapter describes the methods I use, as developed through many years of trial and error. They work well for me, and I hope they'll work for you too.

Rotary cutting basics

Rotary cutting should, in general, be done from a standing position. The vantage point gained by standing and the additional pressure you'll be able to put on the ruler will make for more accurate cutting. If possible, use your rotary cutter on a table that you can walk all the way around. This will minimize the number of times you have to move the fabric you're cutting.

All fabric should be free from wrinkles prior to cutting. This is essential to accurate cutting, so take the time to press your fabric before you work with it.

safety first!

Before we start with cutting, let's talk about safety. Rotary cutter blades are very sharp and can cut you as easily as they cut fabric. Most cutters have a button to lock the position of the blade, and it's a good idea to get in the habit of using it. As you cut, keep all your fingers on the hand that's not holding the cutter on top of the ruler and out of the path of the cutter.

important tip!

Craftsmanship is important, but don't forget that quilt-making is supposed to be fun and relaxing, and don't hesitate to try new things. The more you quilt, the more you'll develop your own unique style and process.

NOTE

These instructions are written for right-handed people, and the photos show a right-handed person cutting. If you're left-handed, you'll want to do the opposite of what is described here, including moving the rotary cutter blade to the opposite side of the cutter.

Unless otherwise noted in the directions, the ruler should always be lined up with the grain of the fabric. Hold it firmly in place with your left hand, keeping all your fingers on top of the ruler and out of the path of the cutter.

Prepare to cut by lining up the blade with the right edge of the ruler. Use even pressure to run the cutter along the edge of the ruler, making a clean cut through the fabric. As you cut, keep your fingers clear of the blade.

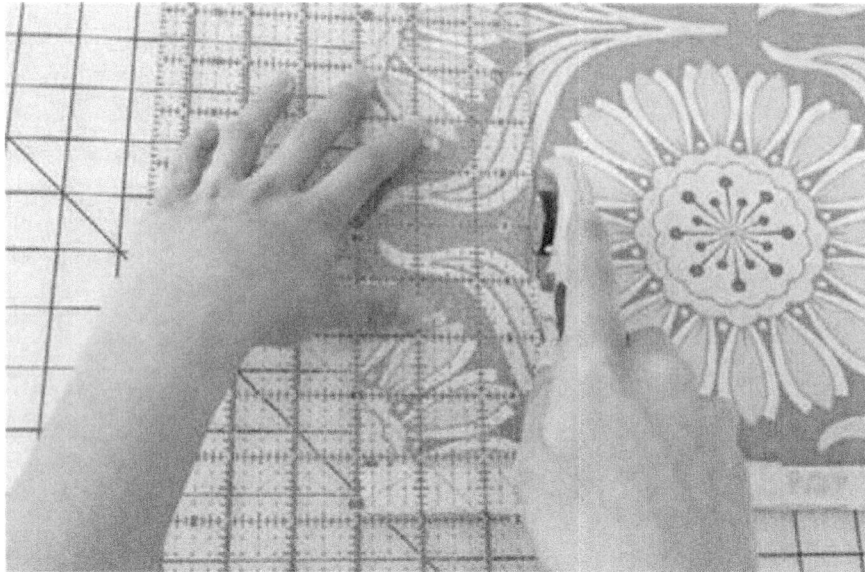

Change your rotary cutter blade regularly. Dull or nicked blades make accurate cutting more difficult and can cause ugly little pulls in the fabric. If it takes more than one pass with the cutter to get though the fabric, it's time to change the blade.

The first cuts you make from your fabric will usually be strips cut along the width or the length of the fabric. In most cases these strips are then cut into smaller pieces.

Cutting along the width (selvage to selvage) is easier and is how most pieces are cut. Cutting along the length (cut edge to cut edge) of the fabric is used to make longer sashing or border strips or backing pieces.

Cutting along the width of the fabric

1. Fold the fabric selvage to selvage and place it on the cutting mat with the folded edge nearest you.

2. Lay a 6″ × 24″ ruler on top of the fabric. Match a horizontal line on the ruler to the fold and slide the ruler near the cut edge on the right side of the fabric.

3. Cut off a small strip of fabric along the right side of the ruler, creating a straight edge at a right angle to the fold. This is called "squaring up" the fabric.

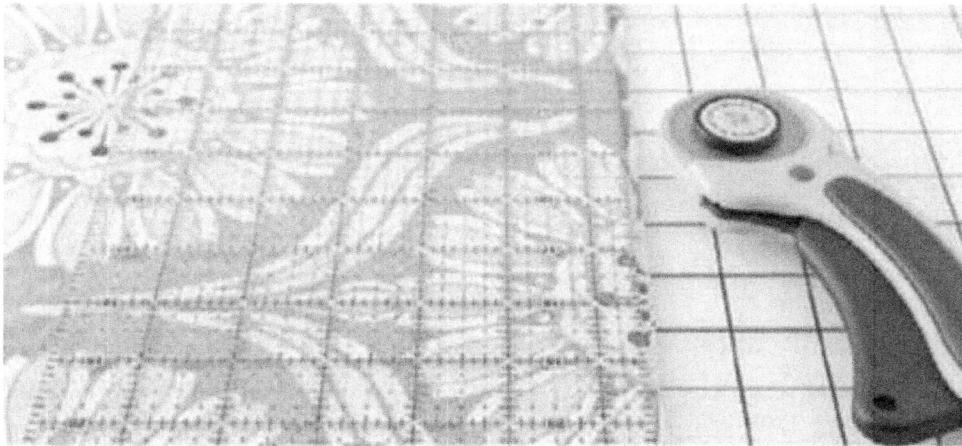

4. Move to the opposite side of the table (or, if you cannot, carefully turn your rotary cutting mat around). Now the straight edge you just cut is on the left side of the fabric, and the folded edge away from you.

5. Use the lines on the ruler to measure the width of the strip you want to cut and, again, cut along the right side of the ruler. Continue making cuts, moving from left to right across the fabric.

Cutting along the length of the fabric

Since fabric is usually about 42″–44″ wide, strips longer than this need to be cut along the length of the fabric (parallel to the selvage edge). To make an accurate cut, you'll first need to refold the fabric to a size that will fit on your mat.

Instead of folding the fabric along the existing fold, fold it in the opposite direction, bringing the cut edges together and matching the selvages along one side. Fold the fabric once or twice more, continuing to keep the selvages along one side lined up, until you can easily lay the fabric on your cutting mat.

You may need to let one end of the fabric hang off the end of the table. Just be careful not to let its weight pull the nicely folded edge out of alignment. You may need to set a book or something else heavy on the folded fabric, out of the way of your cutting tools.

Trim away the selvage to square the edge and use this as the straight edge to cut the pattern pieces. You'll be cutting through more layers than you would if you were cutting along the width, so be careful and realign the edge of the fabric as necessary.

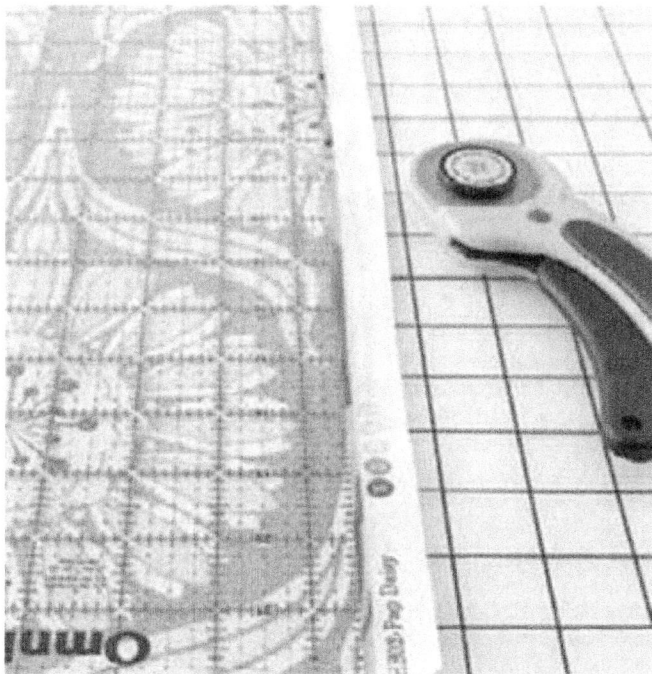

WHAT IF MY RULER ISN'T WIDE ENOUGH?

Some of the patterns require larger pieces than you'll be able to cut with a 6″ × 24″ ruler alone. In those cases, use a 12½″ square ruler to add extra width. When you do this, always keep the 6″ × 24″ ruler on the right edge of the square ruler and cut along the narrow ruler's 24″ edge.

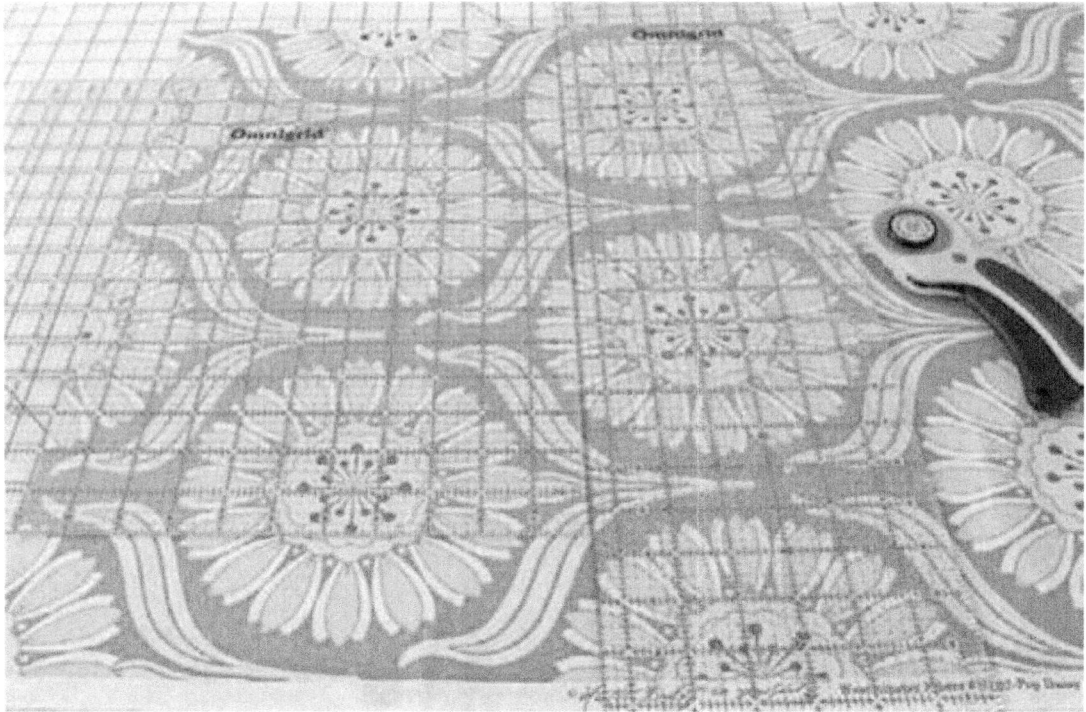

Fussy cutting

Fussy cutting is the common term for cutting a print fabric in such as way as to center or otherwise highlight a particular part of the print.

Cut a piece of translucent template plastic (available at most quilt or craft shops) in the size of the piece you need and move it around the surface of the fabric until you find the part you want to highlight. Keep in mind that when you stitch the piece, you'll lose ¼″ on each side to the seam allowance.

Trace around the outside of the template with a disappearing-ink marker and use the marked lines to cut out the piece with either scissors or a ruler and rotary cutter.

Because you're using only certain parts of the print, fussy cutting takes up quite a bit more fabric than standard rotary cutting. How much more depends on the print, but, in general, I recommend buying twice as much of any fabric that you plan to fussy cut.

Patchwork piecing basics

The patterns I've created for this book reflect my preference for hard edges and sharp, precise piecing. In order to achieve this look, it's important to remember that every step of the process matters. The accuracy of your seam allowances, the way you press the seams, and whether or not you square up your blocks are all-important to duplicating this look.

However, there is absolutely no reason you can't take a more relaxed approach. If you prefer a wonky look or just aren't too concerned about having seams match up exactly, go for it! If you do go this route, keep in mind that your blocks will probably end up being different sizes than mine, so I recommend waiting until after you finish the blocks to cut out any sashing pieces.

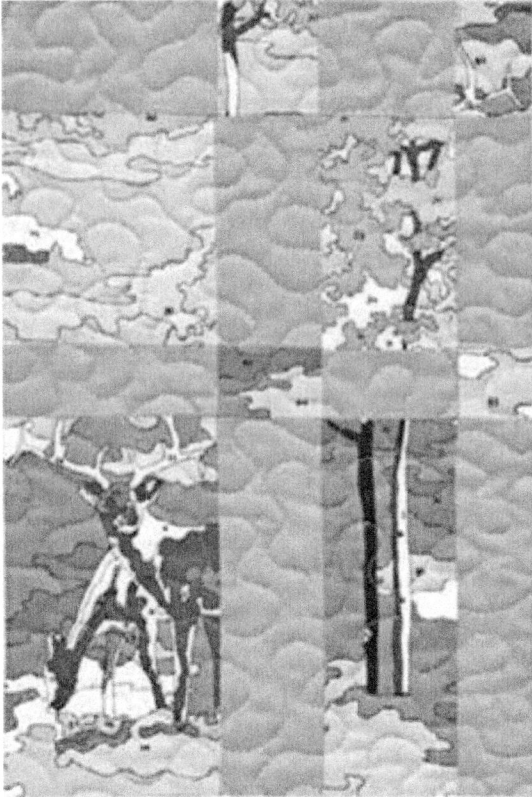

Detail of *Batch of Brownies* (full quilt on page 62)

Seam allowance

Have you ever followed a quilt pattern only to discover that your finished blocks were smaller or larger than they should be? This was most likely caused by a too-wide or too-narrow seam allowance.

Learning to sew an accurate seam allowance is one of the keys to successful patchwork piecing. Most quilt patterns, including the ones in this book, call for a ¼″ seam allowance. Many quilters use the edge of the presser foot as a guide, but beware that foot sizes vary, and yours may not be exactly ¼″ wide.

Before you start any projects, practice sewing seam allowances on some scrap fabric. Sew together 2 squares 2″ × 2″, press the seam open, and measure the pieced unit. When you have an exact ¼″ seam allowance, the pieced unit will measure exactly 2″ × 3½″. If you're having trouble getting it right with the regular presser foot, you may need to switch to a ¼″ seam foot—a special foot with a fabric guide along one side. Alternately, you can use a ruler and blue painter's tape to measure and mark a guideline on your machine's throat plate. Practice until you find what works best for you.

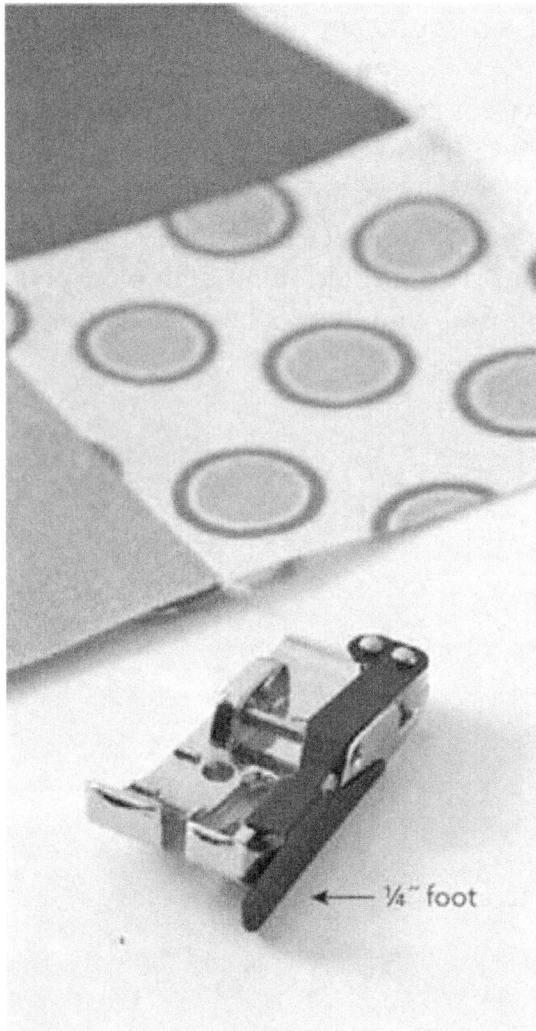

← ¼" foot

Stitch quality

Sew the patchwork pieces together using a small to medium stitch length. I prefer the 2 to 3 setting on my machine, which appears to be about 12 stitches per inch. Before you start sewing on your quilt fabric, test your machine's stitch on scrap fabric and make adjustments if necessary.

In general, if the top of your project looks puckered and the bobbin thread appears to be pulled in a straight line, the thread tension is too tight. If the top thread and bobbin thread are loopy, the thread tension may be too loose. I recommend consulting your machine's manual when making tension adjustments.

BEFORE YOU ADJUST THE TENSION …

If my stitch is bad, the first thing I do is to change my needle. Always. Even if I haven't been using that needle for very long. (Sometimes even a brand-new needle can create poor-quality stitches.) Needles do a lot of work, and even the smallest nick can affect their performance.

Another thing to check is the thread. I cannot stress enough the importance of using quality thread. Switching to a better thread can make a huge difference in stitch quality.

Last but not least, check the bobbin. Take out the bobbin casing and make sure there are no loose threads caught around it. Make sure the bobbin is wound properly and then place it back in the machine.

Pinning

I pin pretty much everything before I sew it, inserting pins through all the layers on both sides of each seam allowance. If there's a large space between seam allowances, I place a pin or two there as well.

Keep a pincushion next to your machine and remove pins as you sew. All this pinning may seem tedious, but it will lead to accuracy.

tip

When sewing together a solid piece of fabric (for instance, a piece of sashing) and a pieced block, always keep the pieced block on top. This will help you keep an eye on the block's seam allowances and ensure that they don't get pulled askew by your machine's feed dogs.

Chain piecing

A great way to save both time and thread, chain piecing is sort of like running a mini assembly line. Gather similar pairs of pieces and run them through your machine one after the other without stopping to clip the threads between pieces. When you're done, clip the threads between each set and press as usual.

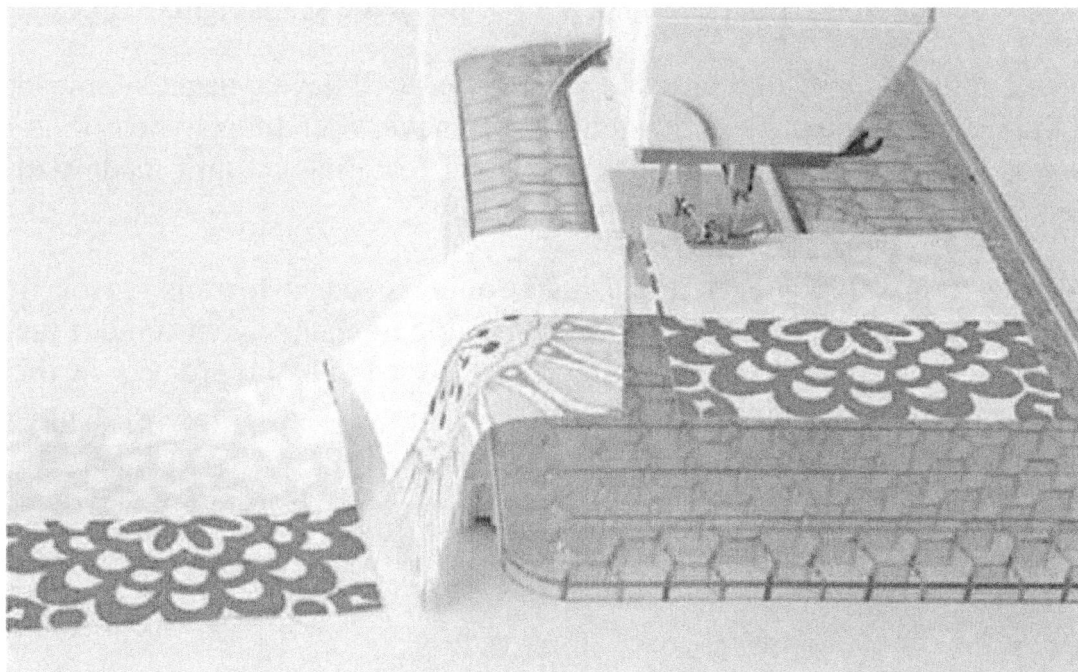

Pressing seams

I press my seams open. It takes a bit more effort than pressing to the side, as many quilters do, but I think the results are worth it. Your finished blocks will be more precise, will lie flatter, and will be easier to machine quilt in an allover pattern. The even distribution of the seam allowances should also ensure that the quilt wears more evenly.

Lay your work right side down on the pressing surface and use your index finger to press open the seam. Follow this by running the point of your iron down the seam. Then place the entire iron over the seam and press firmly, adding a little burst of steam. Flip the work over and gently iron the front (right) side.

For long seams, I usually lay my work faceup on the pressing surface, press to one side, and then flip the project over to press the seam open.

Some quilters believe that pressing seams open will have a negative impact on the structural integrity of the quilt. I have never found this to be true. As long as you're using a good stitch and good materials, a quilt made with pressed-open seams should be perfectly sturdy.

Pressing to the side is easier, and many quilters like it for this reason. If you're a devoted side presser, I may not be able to change your mind. I just encourage you to give open pressing a try, as I think the projects in this book (and modern quilts in general) will be most successful with open pressing.

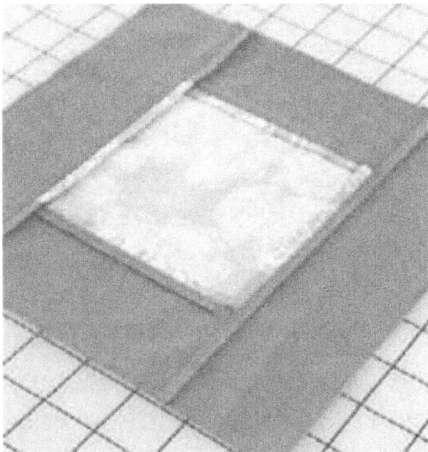

Special piecing techniques

The projects in this book span a wide range of both traditional and contemporary piecing techniques, from the strip piecing used in *Snapshots* (page 51), to the quarter-square triangles in *Planetarium* (page 82), to the wonky Log Cabins in *Sunspot* (page 96), and so on. My hope is that you can learn a new, different, or otherwise interesting technique from each project.

Making a quilt sandwich

Because it takes some floor space, many of us end up doing this step in a different part of our home than we normally use for sewing. Even though I have a sewing room, I find this step always involves shuffling furniture, hauling supplies into another room, and chasing away inquisitive cats. It's worth it though, as taking the time to make a good quilt sandwich will make the next step—machine quilting—go much more smoothly!

1. Start by laying out the batting on a clean, smooth floor. Spread the quilt top on the batting, smoothing out any wrinkles. (You may need to actually crawl on top of the quilt to do this.) Trim the batting to within about 2″ of the quilt top. (A)

2. Starting at the top of the quilt, carefully roll the layered batting and quilt top into a roll. (B)

3. Continue rolling until the batting is completely rolled up, and set it aside with the cut edge down. Don't worry about pinning the batting roll. The natural tendency of most battings is to cling to fabric, so the roll should hold itself together without any help from you.

4. Now spread the quilt backing on the floor, with the right side down. Starting at the bottom of the quilt, use a strip of painter's tape to secure the edge of the quilt back to the floor. Move to the opposite (top) side and, pulling the quilt back ever so slightly toward you, tape the center top to the floor as well. Repeat with the left and right sides and each of the 4 corners, each time pulling very gently, but not stretching, to make sure the quilt back is completely smooth. (C)

5. Bring back the batting roll and, starting at the bottom of the quilt back, slowly unroll the batting and quilt top onto the taped backing. You should have a few inches of leeway on all sides, but you want to make sure that (a) all parts of the quilt top are inside the edges of the quilt back and (b) the rows of blocks in the quilt top are perpendicular to the sides of the quilt back. (D)

A. Spread the quilt top on the batting, smoothing out any wrinkles.

B. Roll the layered batting and quilt top into a roll.

C. Secure the edge of the quilt back to the floor.

tip

This is your only chance to get the alignment right, so if you see that it's off, don't hesitate to reroll the batting and start over!

6. Once again, smooth out the quilt top and batting. I usually do this by starting at the bottom and crawling up the center of the quilt, smoothing as I go. You want to make things smooth, but be careful not to warp the fabric as you work. If you notice that your smoothing is making the blocks wonky, ease up a little bit and work them back into a nice gridded shape.

7. Starting in the center of the quilt and using curved safety pins, pin through all the layers (top, batting, and bottom). I recommend placing pins in a grid pattern, with a pin about every 6″. You can definitely use more pins, but keep in mind that you will have to remove the pins as you quilt, so an excessive number of pins may hamper your quilting progress. (E)

tip

Placing the pins can be tricky at first, but it's something you'll probably get a feel for with practice. Let the pin do the work; just gently guide it through the layers, stopping when it touches the floor. Using too much force on the pin may distort the layers and scratch your floor. If you find opening and closing the pins to be difficult, having a pair of tweezers or needle-nose pliers on hand can be helpful.

8. Once you've finished pinning, remove the tape and trim the quilt backing to the same size as the batting.

You'll want to handle the quilt sandwich with some care. However, if you've done a good job with smoothing and pinning, you should be able to flip the sandwich over and have the back be as smooth and even as the front.

D. Unroll the batting and quilt top onto the taped backing.

E. Pin through all the layers.

Machine quilting basics

Quilting adds texture and beauty to the finished project. It also, quite literally, holds it all together!

If you're nervous about machine quilting, you may be relieved to learn that there are services that will do it for you. If you're concerned about inadvertently damaging that beautiful top (or if you just don't have enough time), sending your project out to a professional quilter may be a good option. Local quilt shops can be excellent resources for finding quilting services.

If you want to finish your quilt at home but aren't sure about doing it on your machine, you might also consider hand quilting. A good resource is

Hand Quilting with Alex Anderson, available from C&T Publishing.

Of course, I recommend learning to machine quilt at home! All the projects in this book were quilted on a regular home sewing machine using one of two basic techniques: *straight-line quilting* using a walking foot or *free-motion quilting* using a darning foot.

Both of these techniques are easy to learn, but don't expect your first attempt to be perfect. Grab a seam ripper and the beverage of your choice, put on your favorite music, and begin quilting with a relaxed attitude. The more you practice, the easier quilting will become and the more polished your finished projects will look. Keep in mind that while you will have been staring at your quilting stitches for hours, the recipient of the quilt is unlikely to notice those imperfections that seem so obvious to you.

tip

Pushing your worktable against a wall can prevent the quilt sandwich from falling off the back of the table as you work. Use your body to support any part of the quilt that would otherwise hang off the front of the table.

Getting started

For either method, you'll need to place your machine on a sturdy table that is clean and completely cleared of obstructions. One of the keys to moving the quilt sandwich around easily during quilting is keeping all of it on top of the table at all times. Accomplish this by loosely rolling or folding the edges of the sandwich and quilting a small area at a time, refolding as necessary as you work your way across the quilt.

tip

As you quilt, keep a small dish or jar nearby to collect safety pins as you remove them from the quilt sandwich.

I like to start in one corner of the quilt and work my way back and forth across the top until the entire surface is covered in quilting stitches. Other quilters like to start in the center and work their way outward. As long as you've made a stable quilt sandwich, either method should work equally well.

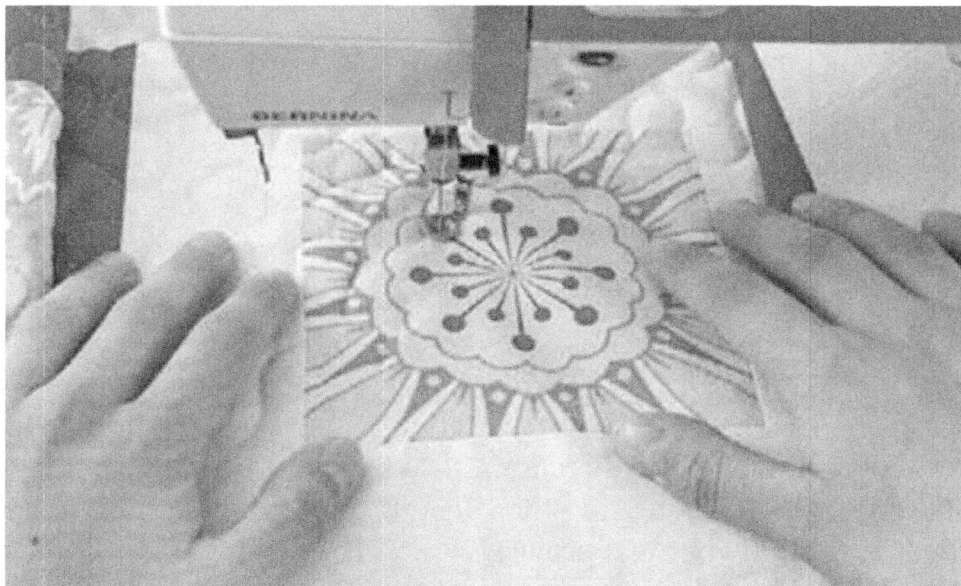

tip

Practice first! Use leftover batting and scrap fabric to make mini quilt sandwiches and practice your planned quilting technique before moving on to the quilt itself.

Quilting with a walking foot

The feed dogs on your sewing machine are like little teeth that cycle up and down under the fabric, pulling it through the machine. This works well when you're sewing through just one or two pieces of fabric, but when it comes time to quilt, your machine needs a little more help. Enter the walking foot. A walking foot adds a second set of feed dogs to the top of the fabric. With feed dogs on the top and bottom, your machine can sew through a quilt sandwich with ease.

Follow the manufacturer's directions to attach the walking foot to your machine. Test the tension and stitch length on a practice quilt sandwich before moving on to your real project.

A walking foot is essential for quilting straight lines. You can do this in a variety of patterns.

Parallel lines

WALKING FOOT IDEAS

PARALLEL LINES

Working from one side of the quilt to the other, sew parallel lines about ½″ apart. Don't worry about keeping the lines perfectly straight or perfectly spaced. These slight differences are part of the charm of a handmade quilt!

LATTICE

Use tailor's chalk or a disappearing-ink marker to draw a lattice pattern on the quilt top and use the lines as a guide for quilting.

RANDOM LINES

For an improvisational look, sew a variety of random lines across the entire quilt top. Keep the lines straight by placing a guide strip of painter's tape across the quilt top before sewing each line.

Lattice

Random lines

AVOID STITCHING IN-THE-DITCH

Stitch in-the-ditch is a technique in which quilters attempt to stitch right along the seams (aka "the ditch") between blocks. The result looks a little like a comforter, which worked well with the puffy polyester battings that were popular in years past. But it doesn't really lend itself to a contemporary aesthetic.

Stitching in-the-ditch also hides from view one of the most beautiful aspects of a quilt—the quilting! If you're looking for a similar style that highlights the shape of the blocks, try outline quilting instead. Rather than quilting right in the seam, use the seam as a guide for the edge of the walking foot and quilt about ¼″ on either side.

Free-motion quilting

Think of your machine's regular settings as the autopilot. The feed dogs pull fabric through as your machine sews regular-sized stitches in a straight line. If you lower or cover the feed dogs and set the stitch length to zero, you disengage the autopilot. This allows you to quilt in a free motion in which the stitch length and shape are determined entirely by the movement of your hands. This is the essence of free-motion quilting. Instead of being restricted to quilting straight lines, you are "free" to quilt in loops, swirls, circles, stars—wherever your imagination leads you.

GETTING YOUR MACHINE READY

Consult your machine's manual for specific information about how to prepare the machine for free-motion quilting. For most machines, you will need to

• fit the machine with a darning or free-motion quilting foot,

• set the machine's stitch length to zero, and

• lower or cover the machine's feed dogs.

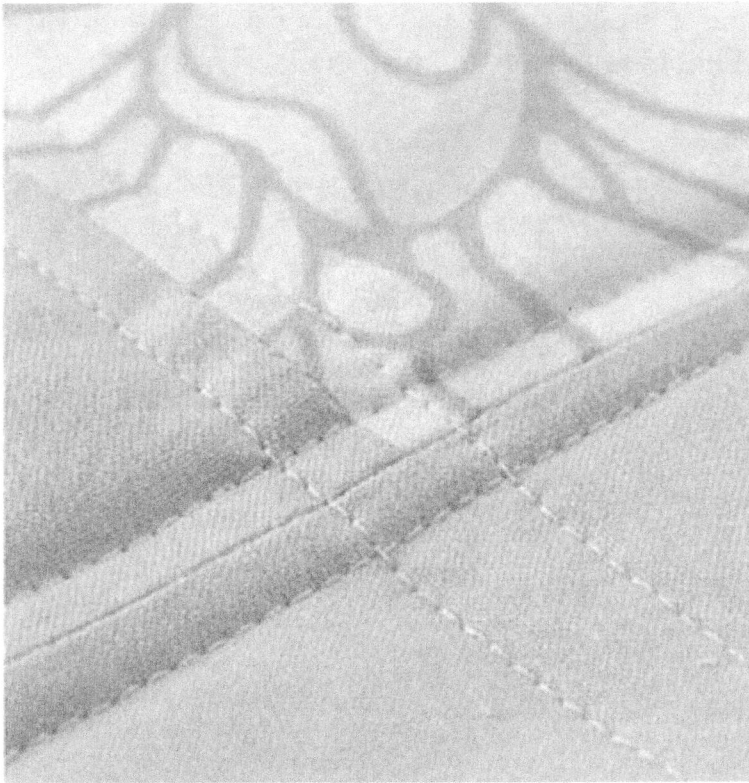

STARTING TO QUILT

1. With your quilt sandwich in the machine, manually bring the needle down and back up again, pulling the bobbin thread through the top of the sandwich. Put the presser foot down. Make several stitches in place to create a knot.

2. Begin to move the quilt sandwich, stitching in your chosen pattern just an inch or so from where you started. Pause, making sure the needle is in the down position, and trim the loose threads so they won't get tangled in your work. Repeat this process every time you run out of thread, always making sure to bring the bobbin to the top and trim the loose ends.

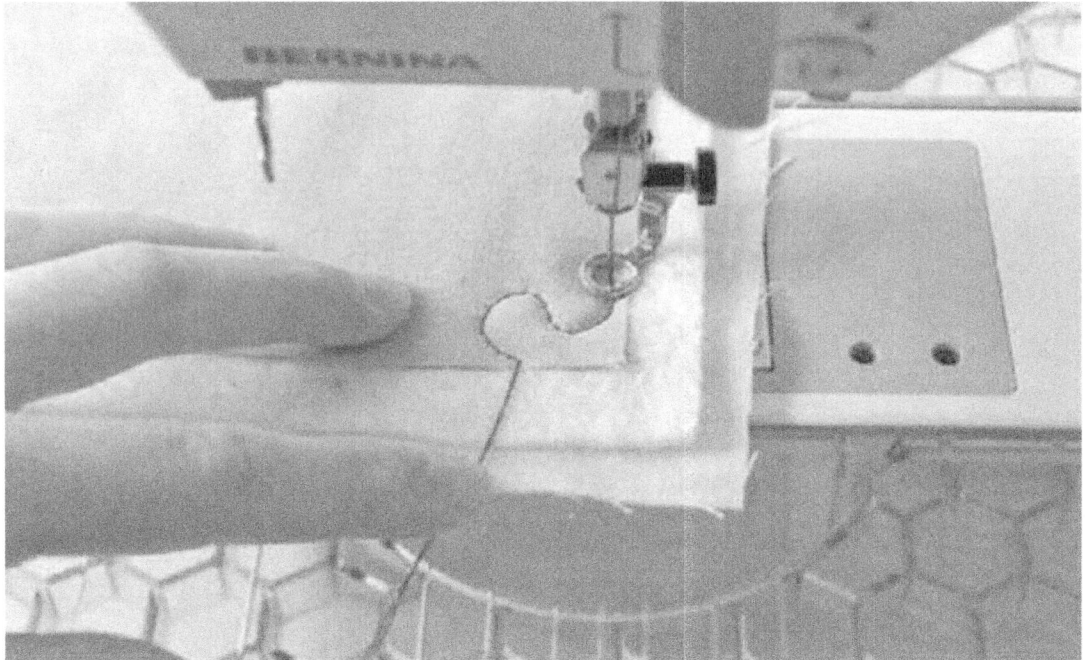

3. Continue quilting, using the motion of your hands to guide the stitching in your desired pattern and removing safety pins as you encounter them.

I find that having a firm grip on the quilt sandwich on both sides of the area I'm quilting is the best way to keep the stitches moving the way I want them to. Other people like to wear rubber gloves (either the dishwashing kind or those made specifically for quilting) and guide the quilt sandwich with their fingertips. Experiment with different grips to figure out what works for you.

As you work, you'll notice that your hands are in control of not only the shape of the stitches, but also their length. If you move too slowly, your stitches will be too short and tight. If you move too quickly, your stitches will be too long and loose.

As you practice, you'll start to get a feel for the right balance between pressure on the pedal and the speed with which you move the quilt sandwich. You may find that pushing the pedal to the ground and moving the quilt sandwich as fast as you can nets the best results, or you may prefer to move more slowly. Practice until you find a balance that works for you.

tip

Tension problems aren't always obvious from the top. Check the quilt back regularly to make sure that your stitches look good on both sides.

tip

It may help to think of the needle and thread as a pen and the quilt sandwich as paper. The twist is that with free-motion quilting, the pen stays in one place while the paper moves beneath it. If you're feeling intimidated, try using this motion to draw prospective quilting patterns with an actual pen and paper. Even if the process is a little different, it can get your hands and mind used to the motion you'll use when you quilt.

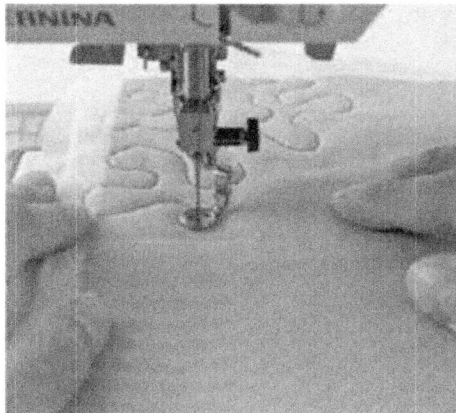

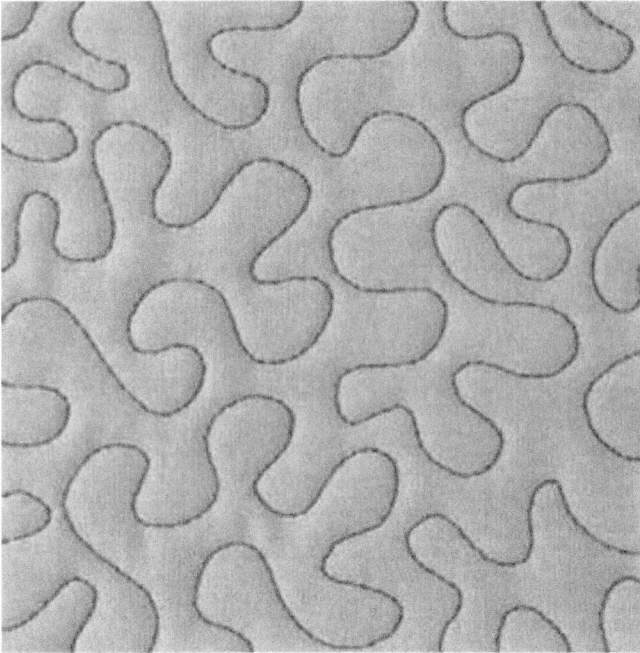

Meandering stitch

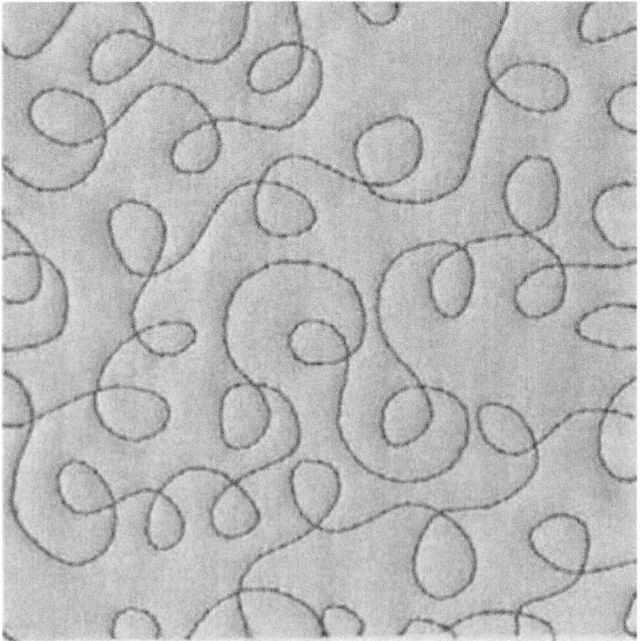

Loopy stitch

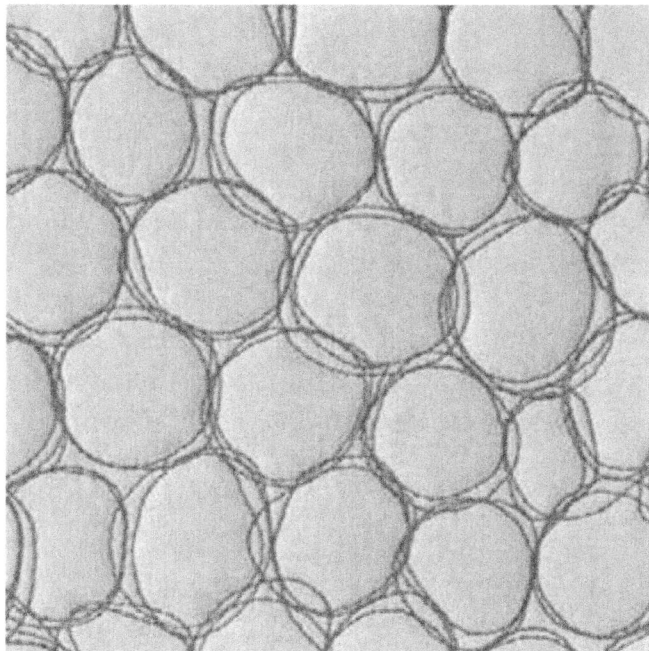

Bubble stitch

FREE-MOTION IDEAS

MEANDERING STITCH

Stitch in a single meandering line that never crosses itself. Quilting with a meandering line in which the stitches are never more than ½″ apart is sometimes called *stippling*.

LOOPY STITCH

Stitch in a single meandering line that loops back on itself at regular intervals.

BUBBLE STITCH

Stitch in a circle, repeating the same circle two or three times before moving on to another circle right next to it. Continue this pattern, filling the surface of your quilt.

Making and sewing binding

Binding is sort of like a frame around the quilt. It's one last place where you can add a pop of color or show off an exciting print.

All the quilts in this book are bound using straight-grain binding, meaning the binding strips are cut along the grain of the fabric rather than on the bias. This method is easier and uses less fabric than making bias binding.

Easy double-fold binding

These steps describe my favorite binding method, which is machine sewn to the quilt and then finished by hand.

1. Sew the binding strips together, end to end, using a ¼″ seam allowance and pressing the seams open. Keeping the wrong sides together, press the entire length of the binding in half. (A)

2. Prepare your quilt for binding by trimming all 4 sides even with the quilt top. Start in the center of one side and pin the raw (unfolded) edge of binding to the edge of the quilt. When you reach a corner, fold the binding up at a 45° angle. (B)

A. Sew the binding strips together.

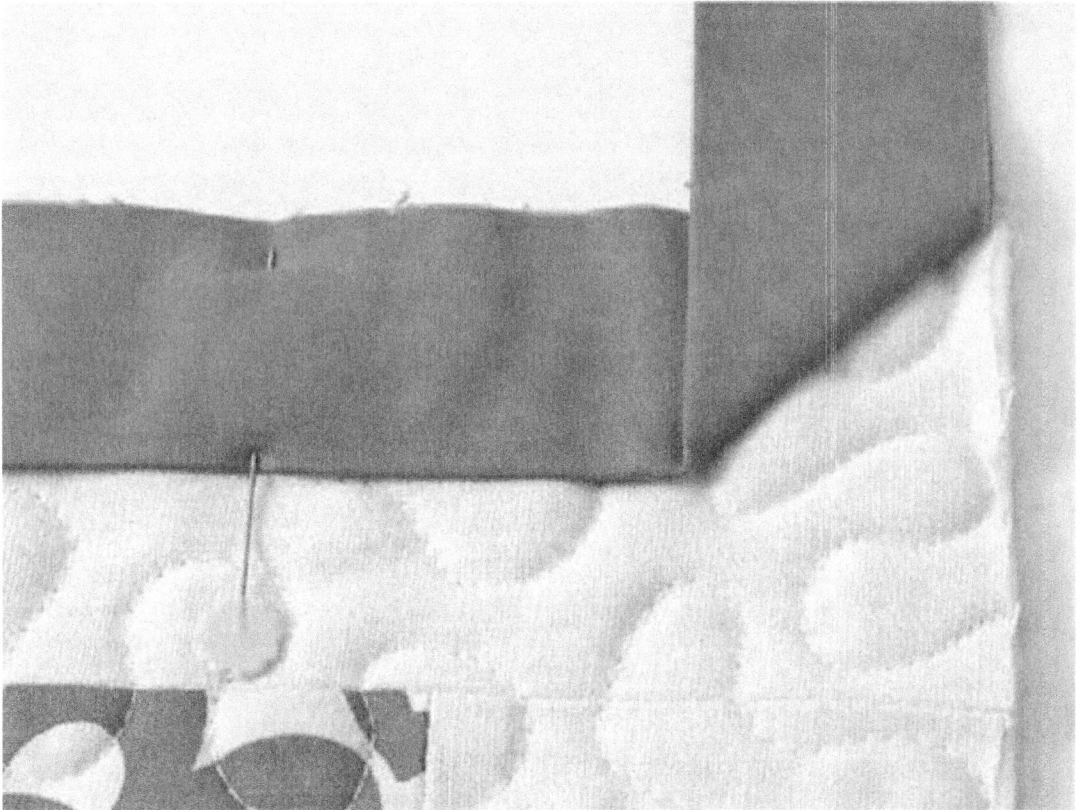

B. Pin the raw edge of the binding to the edge of the quilt. When you reach a corner, fold the binding up at a 45° angle.

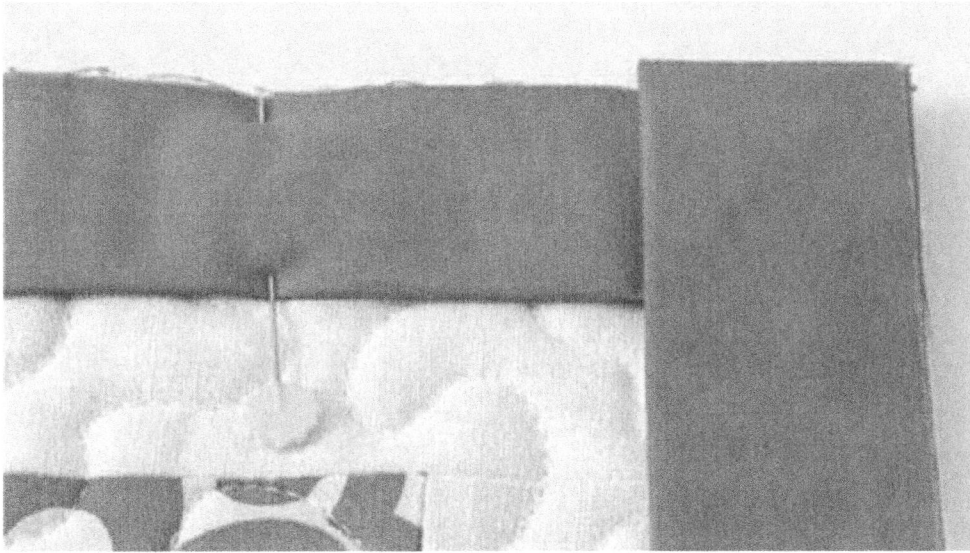

C. Fold the binding back toward the quilt.

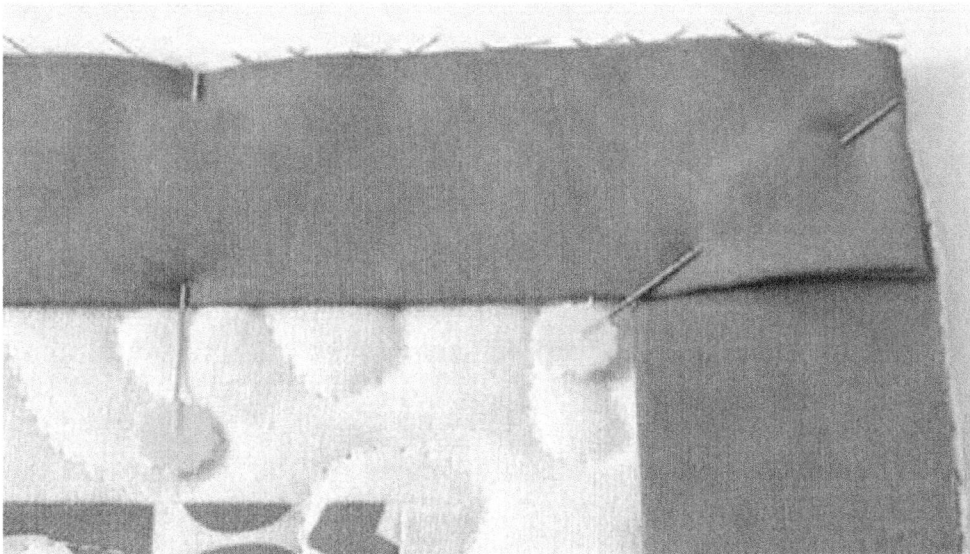

D. Fold down the mitered corner and pin it in place.

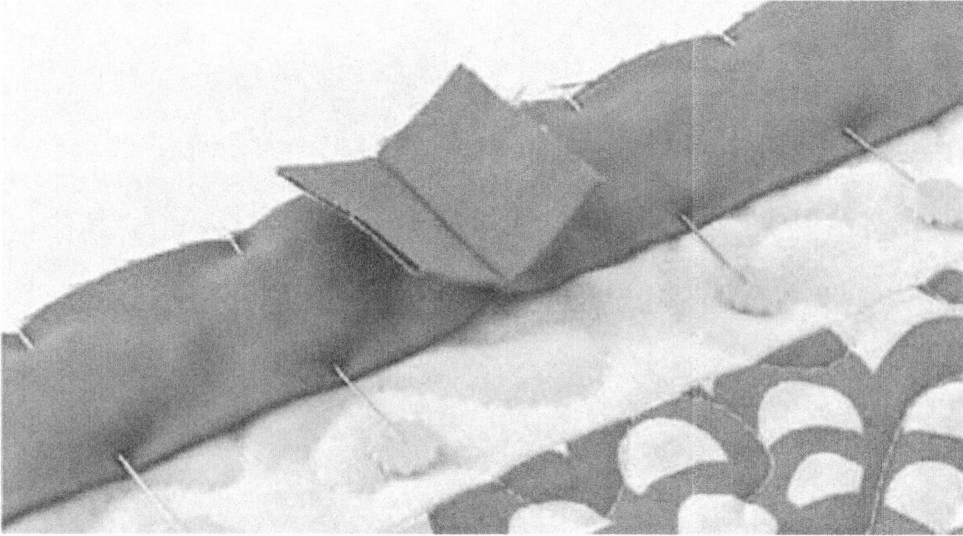

E. Bring both ends of the binding together and press in place.

3. Fold the binding back toward the quilt, creating a mitered corner. (C)

4. Fold the mitered corner down and pin it in place. (D)

5. Continue pinning, repeating Steps 2–4 at each corner until you reach the point where you started. Bring both ends of the binding together, fold each piece back onto itself, and press in place. (E)

6. Trim away any excess binding and use the creases you've just pressed as a guide to sew the ends together. Press the seam open and pin the binding back in place.

You should now have continuous binding pinned all the way around the edges of the quilt sandwich. (F)

7. Use a ¼″ seam allowance to sew the binding to the quilt. When you come to a corner, sew up to but not beyond the miter. Stop, and trim the threads. (G)

8. Fold the mitered corner back. Starting at the corner, continue sewing the binding, repeating Step 7 at each corner, until you reach the point where you started. (H)

9. Fold the binding toward the back of the quilt. The fold you pressed earlier and the mitered corners should make this easy. Use pins or binding clips to secure a section of the binding in place.

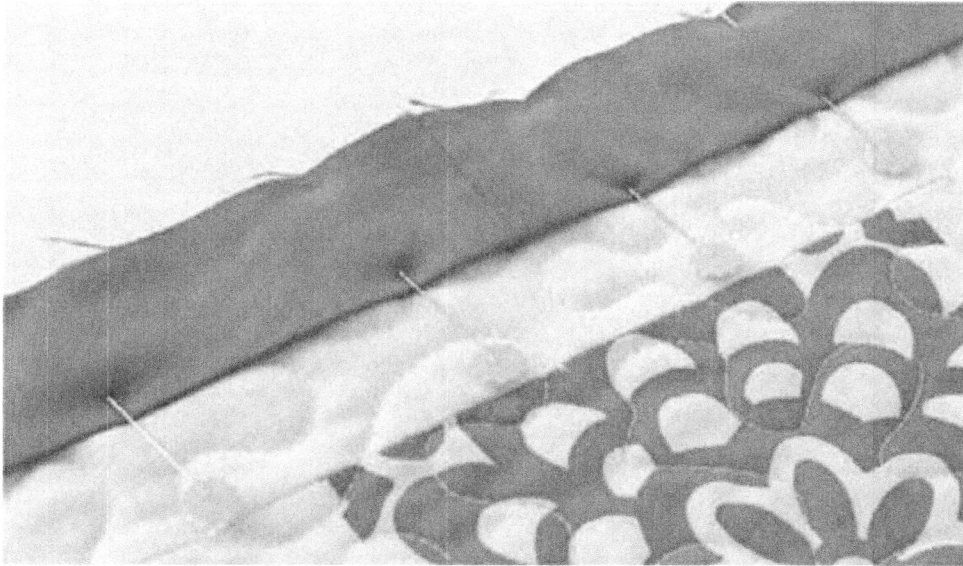

F. Sew the ends together, press the seam open, and pin the binding back.

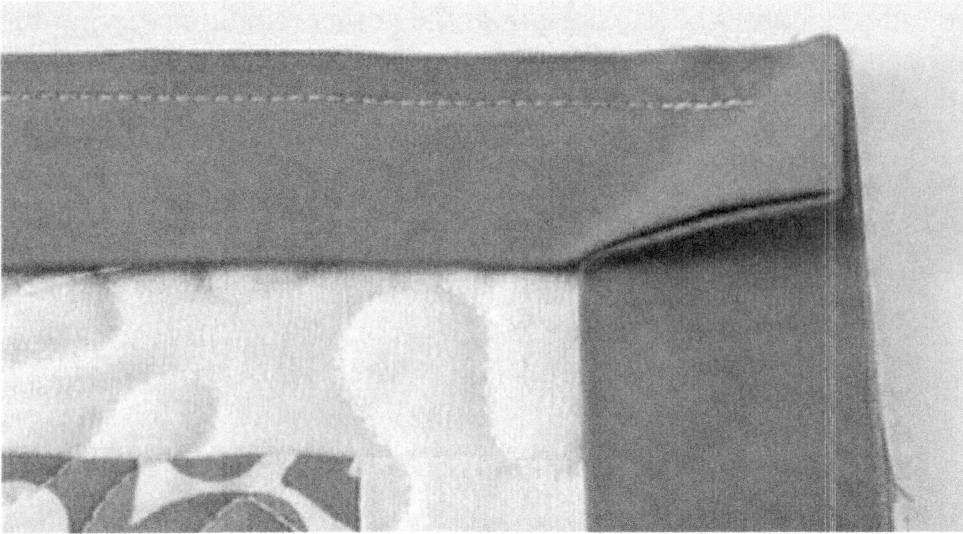

G. Sew the binding to the quilt.

H. Fold the mitered corner back and continue sewing.

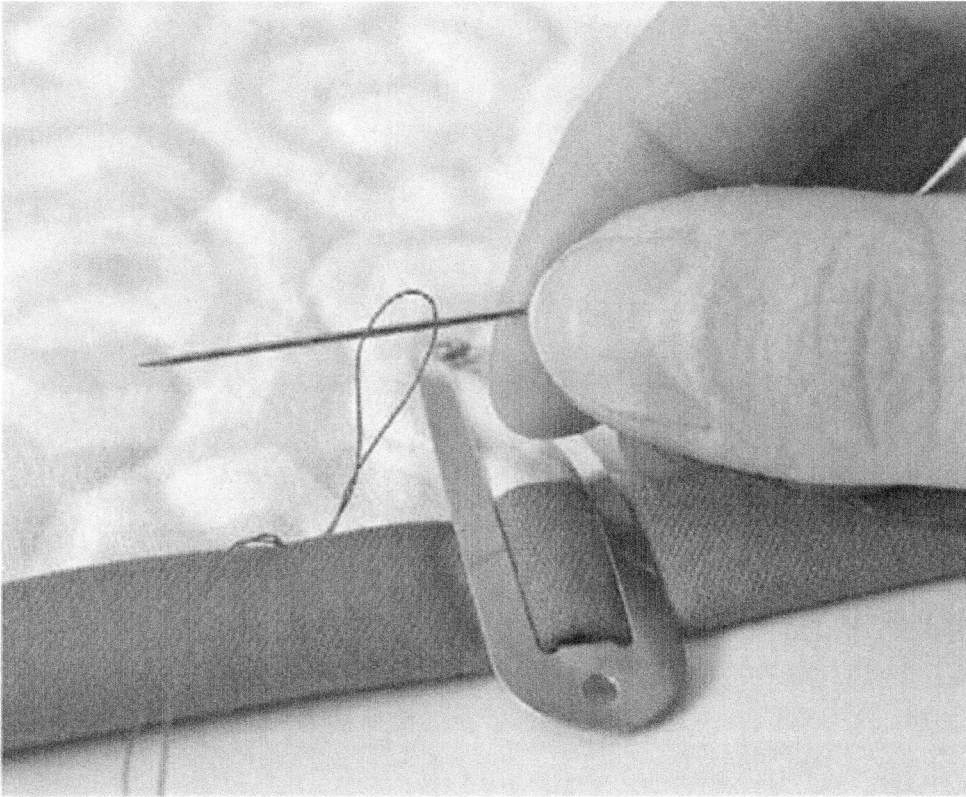

I. Create a knotless start for hand finishing.

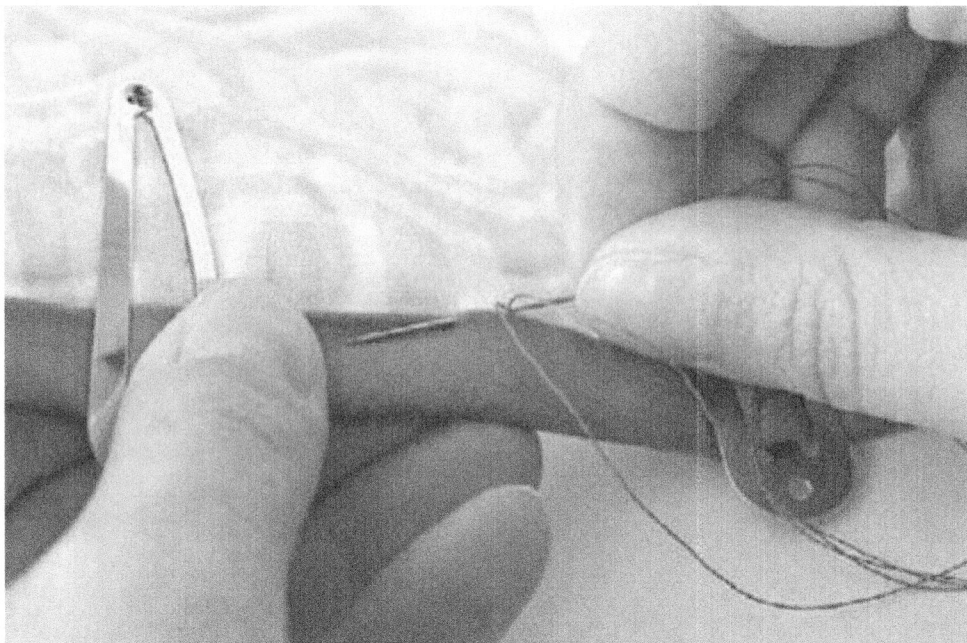

J. Hand stitch the binding in place.

tip

It's not necessary to pin or clip the binding on all sides of the quilt before you start hand sewing. Instead, pin or clip a section approximately 2–3 feet long, pinning the next section only after you've finished sewing the first. This will keep pins and clips from getting caught on your clothes or furniture as you work.

10. To create a knotless start for hand finishing, fold a length of thread in half and thread the folded part through the needle. Pull the loop through so that the 2 loose ends are near the eye of the needle and the loop is at the other end (where a knot would normally be). Pull the needle through the quilt back and batting, near the edge of the binding, leaving the end loop sticking out just a bit. Bring the needle through the edge of the binding and then back through the loop. Continue pulling the needle until the loop closes and the thread is anchored securely. (I)

11. Hand stitch the binding in place, pushing the needle through the quilt back and batting and pulling it back up through the very edge of the binding. Continue sewing, making a stitch about every ¼″. (J)

12. When you reach a corner, continue sewing right up to the edge of the quilt before folding back the mitered corner and continuing on to the next side. (K)

13. Continue until the binding is completely finished. This process can be hard on the tips of your fingers and your fingernails, so if you're concerned about damage, consider wearing thimbles. (L)

tip

Take good care of your finished work. Quilts made with cotton and linen can generally be machine washed and dried. I use cool water, a gentle wash cycle, and gentle detergent, and I tumble dry with low heat.

K. Sew right up to the edge of the corner before folding back the mitered corner

L. Finished binding

A note about the quilt projects

The projects in this book are divided into three chapters, based on the difficulty of the patchwork piecing in each.

If you're a beginner, I suggest starting with one of the simpler projects from the Projects to Get You Started section (page 45). These projects use simple patchwork piecing techniques, and the relatively small number of different-sized pieces in each means that there's less rotary cutting to do.

However, if you're inspired by one of the more complex projects, there's no reason you can't start there. The most important thing is to be realistic. The more complex the project, the more time it will take and the more steps it will involve.

Whichever project you choose, read through all the directions before you start. If you're still not sure about a particular project, try making one or two test blocks with scrap fabric. This may sound like a lot of extra work, but it will make the quilt-making process go much more smoothly!

Following the instructions for each project are sample blocks showing how different fabric choices can alter the entire look of the finished quilt. I've also included alternate fabric requirements and cutting directions for most of the patterns, many of which explain how to substitute precut fabrics for yardage. I hope this will both make the patterns more flexible and get you thinking about how to make your quilting projects more uniquely "you."

Projects to Get You Started

Snapshots by Elizabeth Hartman (see page 51)

Fenced In

Quilt block

Finished Block: 12″ × 12″

Finished Quilt: 76″ × 76″

Made and machine quilted by Elizabeth Hartman.

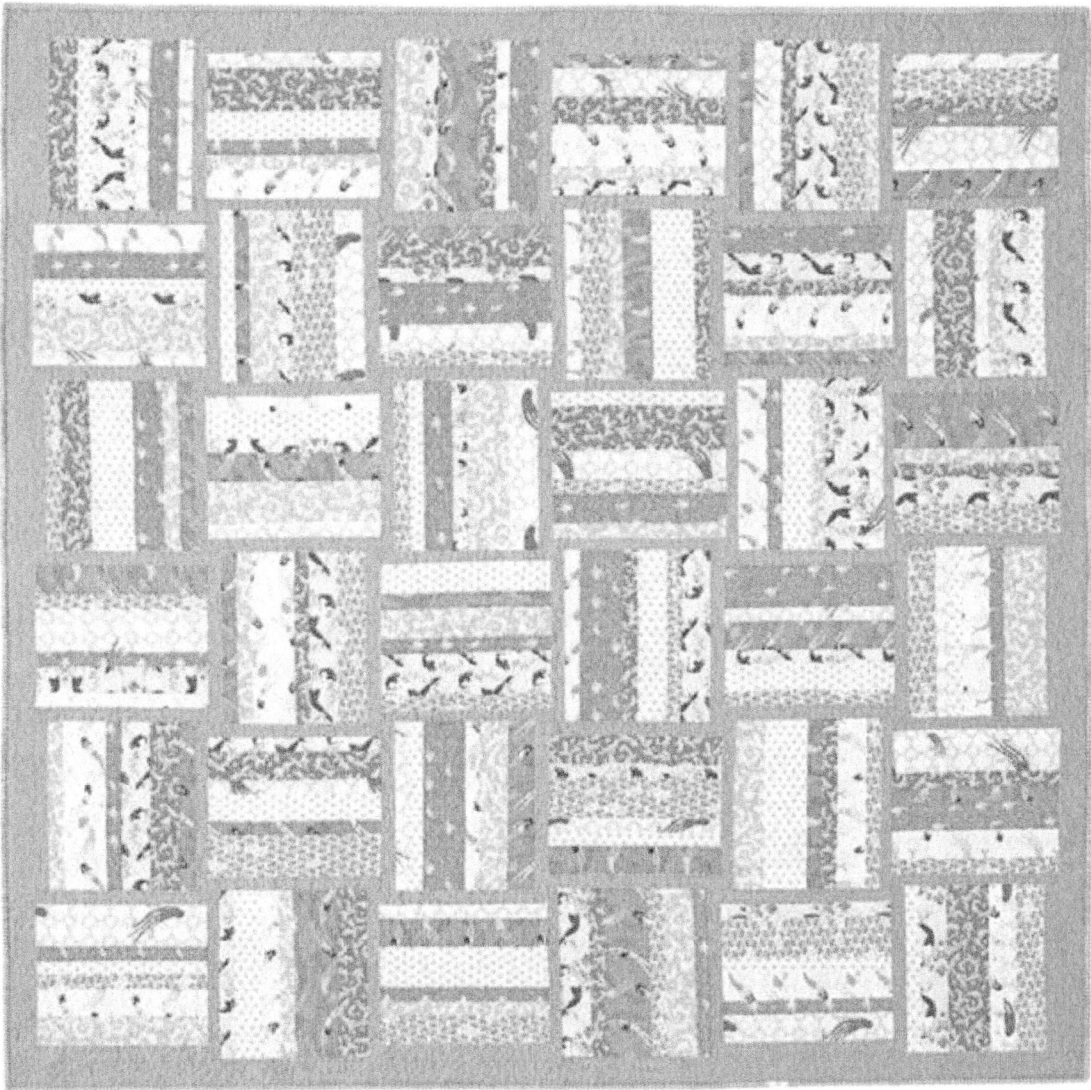

Rail Fence is one of the most basic of traditional quilt blocks. A Rail Fence block is usually a square made of three or four same-sized strips of fabric sewn together. Quilt tops using these blocks are made by rotating every other block 90°, resulting in a zigzag pattern reminiscent of an actual rail fence running across the quilt top.

Each block in this contemporary variation uses a larger number of print fabric strips in a variety of widths. Making the two outside strips on each block from a contrasting solid fabric results in the print fabric strips being "fenced in" by the solid when every other block is rotated.

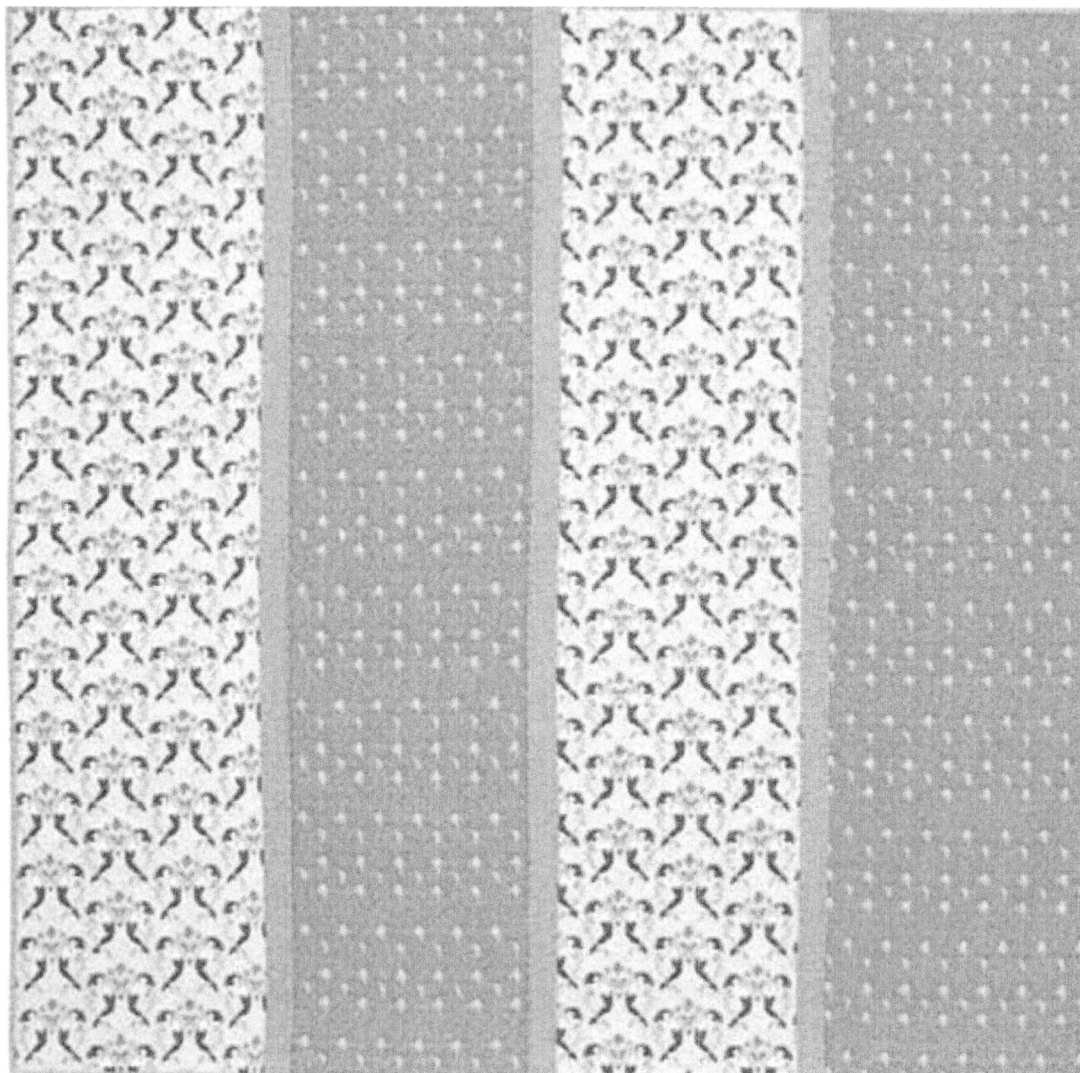

Quilt back

tip

This project calls for cutting fabric along both its length and width. See page 27 for more information about how to do this.

Materials

Yardages are based on fabric that is at least 40" wide. This quilt will be most successful with coordinating prints in a variety of small-, medium-, and large-scale designs.

¾ yard *each* of 9 different print fabrics* for quilt blocks

2⅞ yards contrasting solid fabric for sashing, borders, and quilt back

2½ yards *each* of 1 large-print and 1 small-print fabric for backing

¾ yard binding fabric

80" × 80" batting

36 organizer cards (see page 17)

See More Fabric Options (page 50) for alternate fabric and cutting instructions.

Cutting Instructions

Quilt block print fabrics:

From *each* of the 9 prints, cut:

• 2 strips 12½" × width of fabric

Subcut 1 strip into 4 pieces 3½″ × 12½″ and 8 pieces 2½″ × 12½″.

Subcut the other strip into 12 pieces 1½″ × 12½″.

You should now have the following print fabrics cut for the quilt block construction:

- 36 pieces 3½″ × 12½″
- 72 pieces 2½″ × 12½″
- 108 pieces 1½″ × 12½″

Contrasting solid fabric:

For the sashing, cut:

- 1 strip 12½″ × width of fabric

  Subcut this strip into 24 sashing strips 1½″ × 12½″.

- 1 strip 12½″ × *length* of fabric

  Subcut this strip into 48 more sashing strips 1½″ × 12½″.

You should now have 72 total 1½″ × 12½″ sashing strips.

For the borders and quilt back, cut from the remaining fabric:

- 7 strips 2½″ × *length* of fabric

  Trim 4 strips to 78″ long for the quilt borders. Set aside the remaining 3 strips for the quilt back.

Backing fabric:

From *each* 2½-yard piece, cut:

- 1 piece 17½″ × *length* of fabric
- 1 piece 22½″ × *length* of fabric

Binding fabric:

• Cut 8 strips 2½″ × width of fabric.

Making the Blocks

All seam allowances are ¼″, and all seams are pressed open unless otherwise noted.

1. Lay your organizer cards out on a table, bed, or other large area. Each of these cards will correspond to 1 block in your quilt. Divide the cut strips among the cards, adding the following to each: 1 strip 3½″ wide, 2 strips 2½″ wide, and 3 strips 1½″ wide. Add 2 sashing strips to each card.

2. Working a block at a time, sew the 6 strips into 3 pairs and the 3 pairs into 1 pieced unit 10½″ wide. Vary the arrangement of the different-width strips among the blocks.

tip

Don't worry about where each of the blocks will fit into your finished quilt or in what order these strips will be sewn together. Just concentrate on distributing the colors and patterns evenly.

3. Sew a sashing strip to each side, creating a 12½″ square block. Repeat until all 36 blocks are complete.

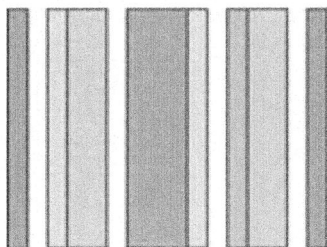

Quilt block assembly diagram. Make 36.

Making the Quilt Top

1. Referring to the quilt top assembly diagram, sew finished blocks into 6 rows of 6 blocks each, rotating every other block 90°. Sew the rows together.

2. Sew 1 border strip to the top edge and 1 to the bottom edge of the quilt top. Trim off the excess border fabric to square the corner.

3. Sew 1 of the remaining border strips to each side to complete the quilt top. Trim excess length from the corners to create a 76½″ × 76½″ square quilt top.

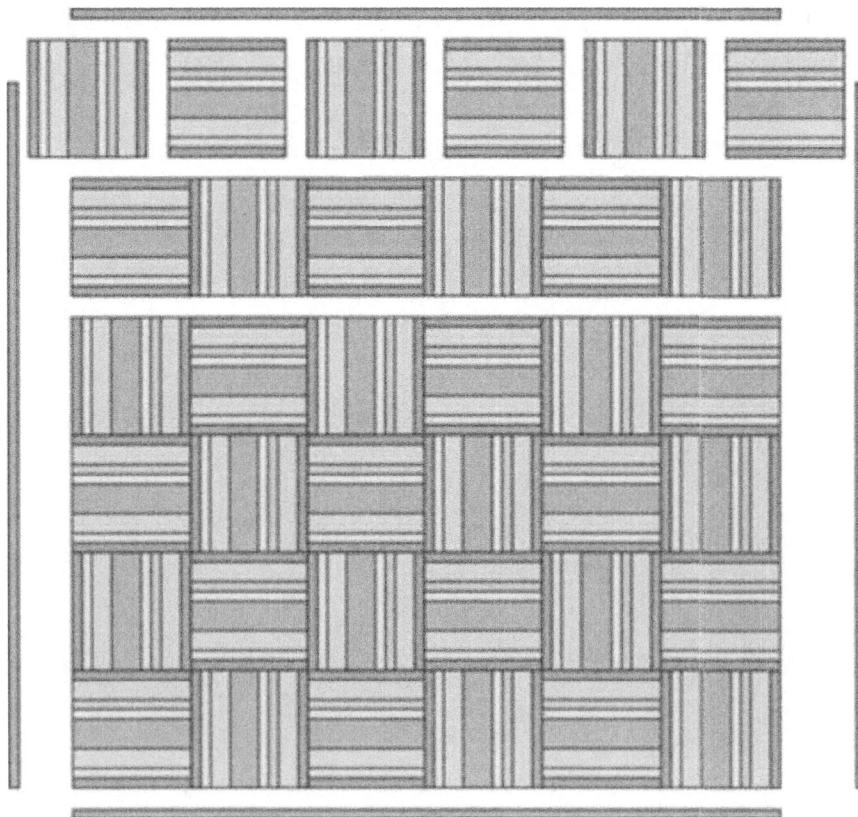

Quilt top assembly diagram

Making the Quilt Back

Sew together the backing pieces as shown in the quilt back assembly diagram. Trim the edges even.

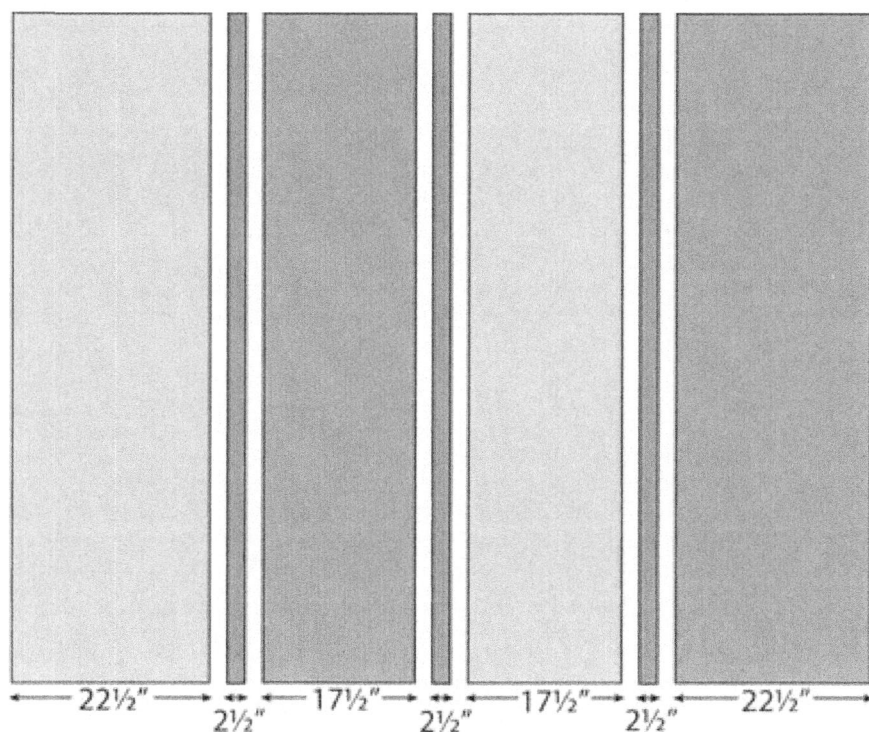

Quilt back assembly diagram

tip

The accuracy of the long seams on the quilt back will go a long way toward making it flat (and the quilt sandwiching process easier!). Use plenty of pins and take your time with these seams, keeping both the seam allowance and stitch quality consistent.

Finishing the Quilt

Refer to Step-by-Step Quilt Construction (<u>pages 25–44</u>) for details on sandwiching, quilting, and binding your project.

Alternate Ideas

MAKE IT SCRAPPY

This is a great project for using all those skinny fabric pieces left over from other projects. You'll need 36 pieces 3½″ × 12½″, 72 pieces 2½″ × 12½″, and 108 pieces 1½″ × 12½″. Divide the scrappy pieces among a set of organizer cards and proceed exactly as the pattern describes.

MAKE IT RANDOM

Is cutting all those different-width strips too fussy for you? Cut and piece the fabric strips at random, trimming the blocks to 10½″ × 12½″ and adding 1½″ neutral sashing strips as the pattern directs. In this example, I've used a neutral sashing and included thin strips of bright solids in the blocks.

More Fabric Options

Use either of the following options as a substitute for the print fabrics used in the quilt blocks:

Option 1: ½ yard *each* of 18 different fabrics

- From *each* of the 18 fabrics, cut 1 strip 12½″ × width of fabric.

  Subcut each strip into:

  2 pieces 3½″ × 12½″

  4 pieces 2½″ × 12½″

  6 pieces 1½″ × 12½″

Option 2: 1 fat quarter *each* of 36 different fabrics

- From *each* fat quarter, cut 1 strip 12½″ × width of fat quarter.

  Subcut *each* strip into:

  1 piece 3½″ × 12½″

  2 pieces 2½″ × 12½″

  3 pieces 1½″ × 12½″

Snapshots

Quilt block

Finished Block: 12″ × 12″

Finished Quilt: 48″ × 60″

Made and machine quilted by Elizabeth Hartman.

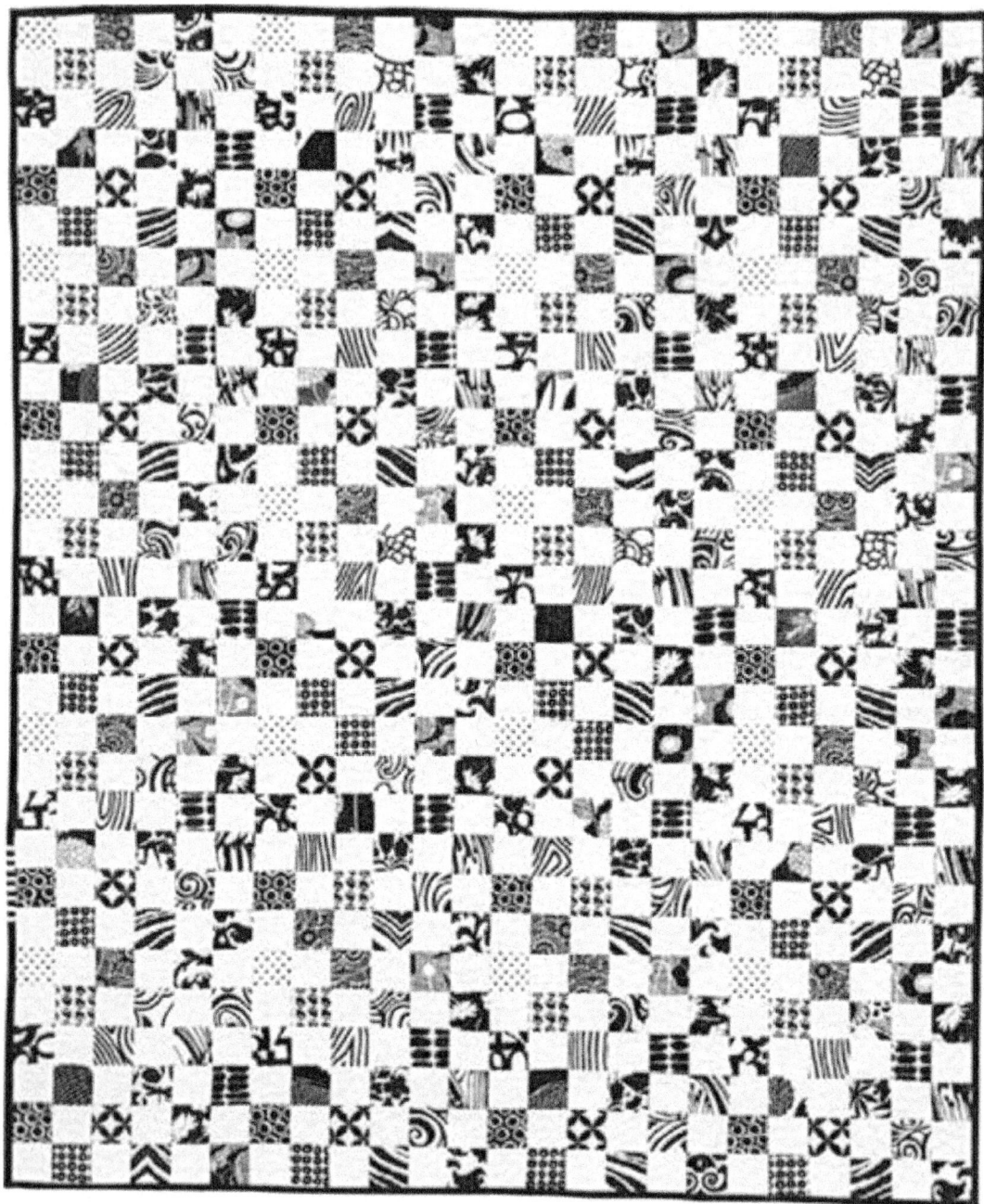

Materials

Yardages are based on fabric that is at least 40" wide.

¼ yard *each* of 18 different print fabrics* for quilt blocks

2¾ yards white (or other neutral solid) fabric for quilt blocks

2 yards contrasting solid fabric, *at least* 42" wide for backing

½ yard binding fabric

52" × 64" batting

See More Fabric Options (page 55) for alternate fabric and cutting instructions.

The 2" squares on this quilt top are like a sea of tiny black-and-white photographs. Piecing this many small squares may seem daunting, but the process is speeded up with a technique called strip piecing.

Instead of cutting all those squares individually, strip piecing (alternately known as quick piecing or speed piecing) involves sewing long strips of fabric together and then slicing them into already-joined rows of squares. Simple!

Using solid white fabric keeps things looking crisp, and a second solid fabric adds a pop of color to the quilt back.

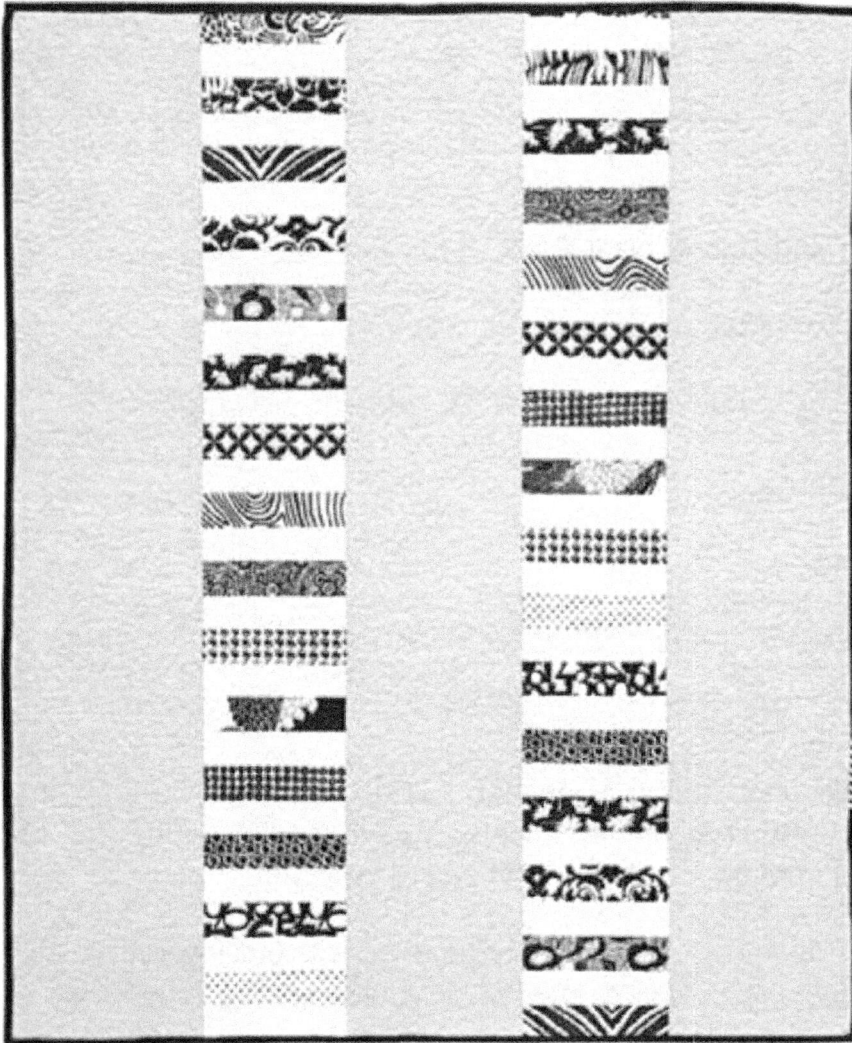

Quilt back

Cutting Instructions

Quilt block print fabrics:

From *each* of the 18 print fabrics, cut 2 strips 2½" × width of fabric.

You should now have 36 total 2½" × width of print fabric strips for the quilt top construction.

Quilt block white or neutral solid fabric:

Cut 36 strips 2½" × width of fabric.

Backing fabric:

From the 2 yards of contrasting solid, cut:

- 1 strip 10½" × *length* of fabric
- 2 strips 15½" × *length* of fabric

Binding fabric:

- Cut 6 strips 2½" × width of fabric.

Making the Blocks

All seam allowances are ¼", and all seams are pressed open unless otherwise noted. Note: If you are using a directional print, see the special tip on page 54.

1. Sew each of the 36 print strips to 1 of the 36 solid strips to form 36 paired strip units.

2. Separate the strip units into 3 random piles (12 units per pile). Sew together 1 unit from each pile, alternately joining solid to print strips, creating 12 strip sets that are each 6 strips wide.

3. Crosscut each strip set into 1 unit 8½″ wide and 10 units 2½″ wide. As you cut, stack the 8½″ units into 1 pile for the quilt back and the 2½″ units into 12 piles of 10 identical units for the quilt front.

You should have a total of 12 units for the back and 120 units for the front. Set aside the 8½″ quilt back units.

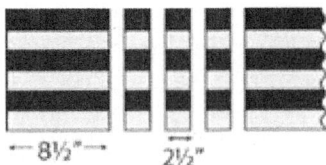

4. Pin and sew pairs of 2½″ strip sets together along the long edges, randomly selecting 1 strip set from each pile and alternating solid and print squares to make a checkerboard pattern. You should have a total of 60 paired strip units.

5. Continue alternating print and solid squares, pinning and sewing together sets of 3 pairs to create 20 blocks as shown in the block assembly diagram.

Block assembly diagram

tip

There are lots of seams to match on this quilt! For maximum accuracy, start pinning in the middle and work your way out.

tip

If you're using directional prints, half of your print strips should be sewn to the left and half to the right of the solid strips. When joining these to make strip sets, half of the sets should have a solid and the other half a print on the left side. When sewing the strip set units into blocks, make sure that the top left square of each block is solid. This should enable you to keep all directional prints oriented properly.

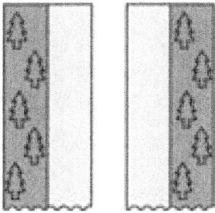

Sew half the print strips on the right and half on the left.

Making the Quilt Top

Alternate the block layouts in a checkerboard pattern, as shown in the quilt top assembly diagram. Sew the finished blocks into 5 rows of 4 blocks each. Sew the rows together to complete the quilt top.

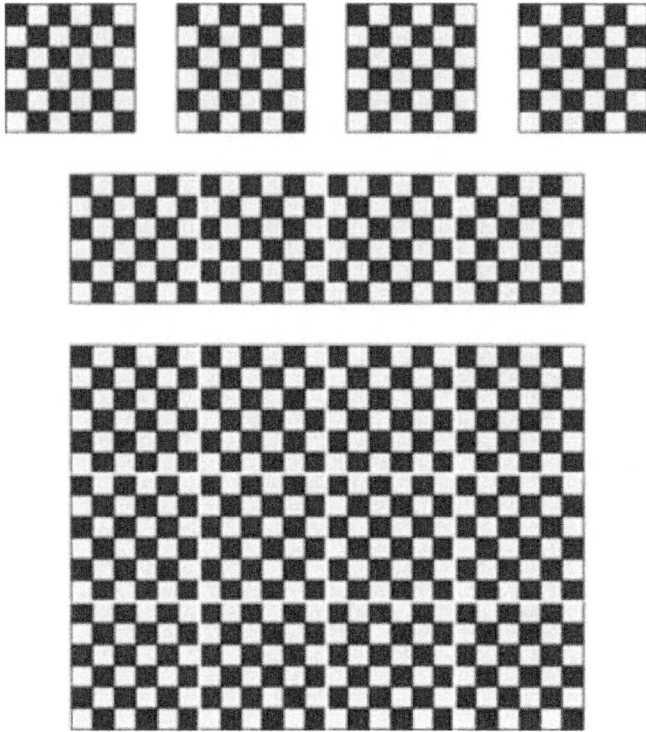

Quilt top assembly diagram

Making the Quilt Back

1. Divide the 8½" quilt back units into 2 sets of 6. Sew each set of 6 units together along the long edges to make a 72"-long strip. Press all the seams open.

2. Sew a pieced strip to each side of the 10½"-wide backing strip.

3. Sew a 15½"-wide backing strip to each side of the section created in Step 2.

4. Trim the edges even.

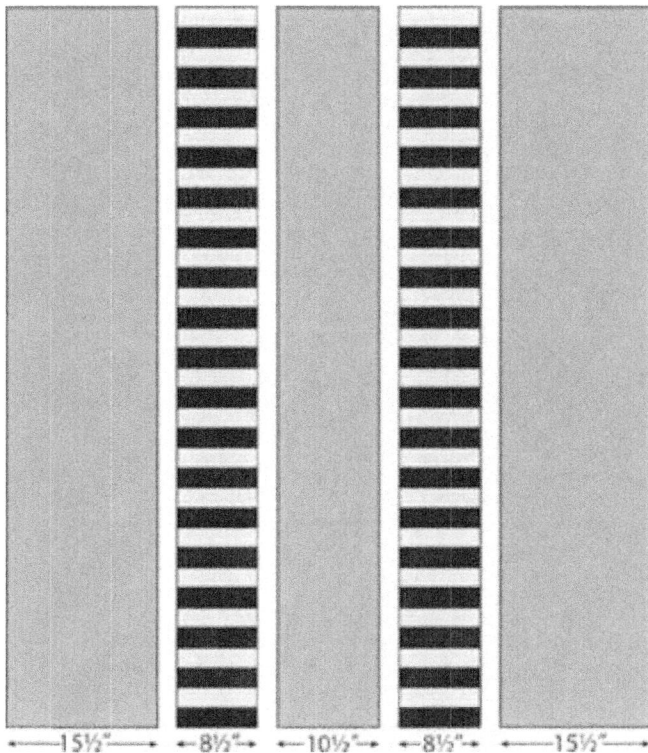

←——15½"——→ ←8½"→ ←—10½"—→ ←8½"→ ←——15½"——→

Quilt back assembly diagram

Finishing the Quilt

Refer to Step-by-Step Quilt Construction (pages 25–44) for details on sandwiching, quilting, and binding your project.

Alternate Ideas

MAKE IT SCRAPPY!

Although it takes a little longer, piecing each block from 18 solid and 18 print squares can be a great way to use those tiny scraps you just can't bear to throw away. This example uses natural linen and a variety of fussy-cut squares.

To make a 48″ × 60″ quilt, you'll need 360 print and 360 solid 2½″ × 2½″ squares for the front and 36 print and 36 solid 2½″ × 8½″ pieces for the back.

MAKE IT DIFFERENT!

Add some visual interest by using not one but several solid fabrics. I used a neutral cream but also added strips of gray, teal, and ruby to liven things up.

More Fabric Options

Use any of the following options as a substitute for the print fabrics used in the quilt top. You'll need 36 total strips 2½" × width of fabric. You can use as many or as few different prints as you want.

Option 1: A precut roll of 36 strips 2½" wide

Option 2: ⅜ yard *each* of 9 different fabrics

• From *each* of the 9 fabrics, cut 4 strips 2½″ wide.

Option 3: ½ yard *each* of 6 different fabrics

• From each of the 6 fabrics, cut 6 strips 2½″ wide.

Small Plates

Print block

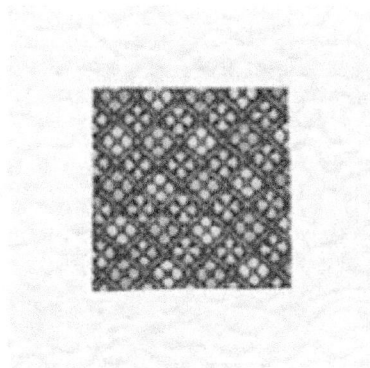

Solid block

Finished Block: 8½" × 8½"

Finished Quilt: 68" × 85"

Made and machine quilted by Elizabeth Hartman.

One of the most tried and true of contemporary patchwork motifs, the Square-in-Square block creates a fabric "frame" around a center square. Not only does it do a great job of showing off your favorite fabrics, but it's also easy to piece, making it a fantastic choice for beginners.

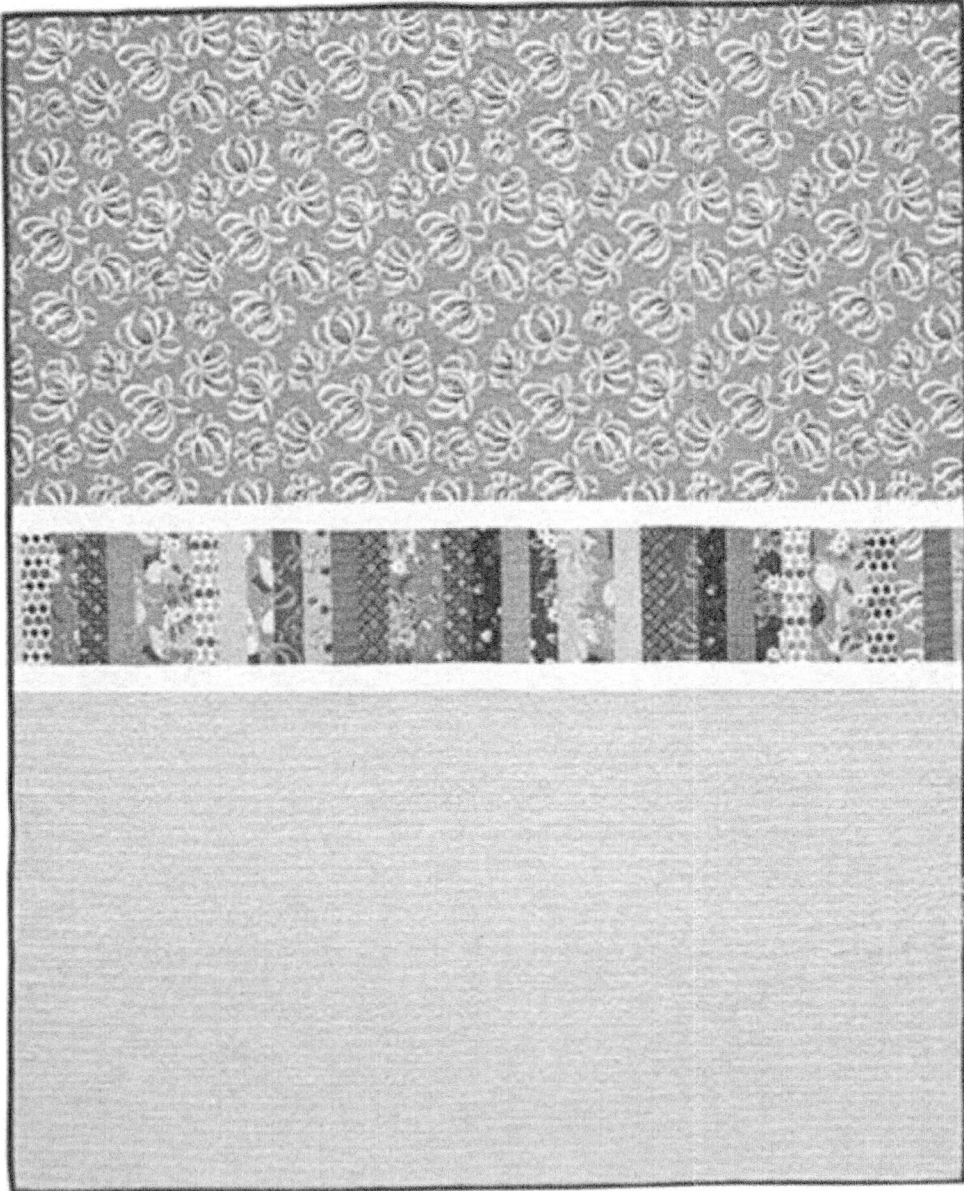

Quilt back

Materials

Yardages are based on fabric that is at least 40" wide, unless otherwise noted.

⅜ yard *each* of 20 different print fabrics[*] for quilt blocks and back

2½ yards neutral solid fabric for quilt blocks and back

2¼ yards *each* of 2 coordinating print fabrics for backing

¾ yard binding fabric

72" × 89" batting

See More Fabric Options (page 61) for alternate fabric and cutting instructions.

Cutting Instructions

Quilt block print fabrics:

From *each* of the 20 print fabrics, cut:

• 2 strips 2½" × width of fabric

  Subcut *each* of these strips into 2 pieces 2½" × 5", 2 pieces 2½" × 9", and 1 piece 2½" × 10".

• 1 strip 5" × width of fabric

  Subcut *each* strip into 4 squares 5" × 5".

You should now have the following print fabrics cut for the quilt construction:

• 80 squares 5" × 5"

• 80 pieces 2½" × 5"

- 80 pieces 2½" × 9"
- 40 pieces 2½" × 10" (for the quilt back)

Neutral solid fabric:

Unfold the fabric and trim off the selvage edges. Then cut:

- 2 strips 2½" × *length* of fabric

  Trim each strip to 2½" × 76½" long.

Refold the fabric along the width, then cut:

- 6 strips 5" × width of fabric

  Subcut the strips to make 80 pieces 2½" × 5".

- 6 strips 9" × width of fabric

  Subcut the strips to make 80 pieces 2½" × 9".

You should now have the following cut from the neutral solid fabric for the quilt construction:

- 80 pieces 2½" × 5"
- 80 pieces 2½" × 9"
- 2 strips 2½" × 76½" (for the quilt back)

Backing fabrics:

From *each* of the 2¼-yard coordinating fabrics:

- Trim off the selvage edges and trim each fabric to measure 76½" long.

Binding fabric:

- Cut 8 strips 2½" × width of fabric.

Making the Blocks

All seam allowances are ¼", and all seams are pressed open unless otherwise noted.

There are 80 blocks in the finished quilt top. Each block is made from a 5" × 5" print square and a set of 2 pieces 2½" × 5" and 2 pieces 2½" × 9". Half (40) of the blocks are made with all print fabrics. We'll call these the print blocks. The other half (40) are made with a print square and solid pieces. We'll call these the solid blocks.

tip

To ensure that the print fabrics are distributed evenly throughout the quilt, make sure to divide the 5" squares equally between the print and solid blocks. For instance, if you have four squares cut from each fabric, use two of them to make print blocks and two of them to make solid blocks.

Making the solid blocks

1. Use 40 of the 5" print fabric squares, 80 solid fabric 2½" × 5" pieces, and 80 solid fabric 2½" × 9" pieces.

2. Sew 2½" × 5" pieces of solid fabric to the top and bottom of each square.

3. Sew 2½″ × 9″ pieces of solid fabric to the right and left sides of each block to finish the block.

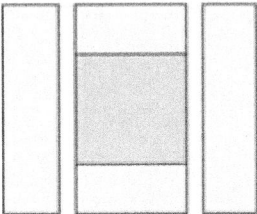

4. Square up each block to 9″ × 9″.

Making the print blocks

1. Use the 40 remaining 5″ print fabric squares, 80 print fabric 2½″ × 5″ pieces, and 80 print fabric 2½″ × 9″ pieces.

2. Pair each 5″ square with a matching set of 2 pieces 2½″ × 5″ and 2 pieces 2½″ × 9″.

3. Sew the 2½″ × 5″ pieces to the left and right sides of each corresponding square.

4. Sew the 2½″ × 9″ pieces to the top and bottom to finish each block.

5. Square up each block to 9″ × 9″.

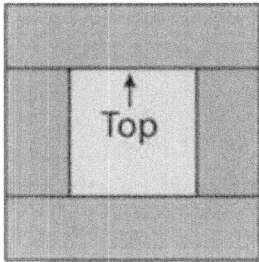

Print block

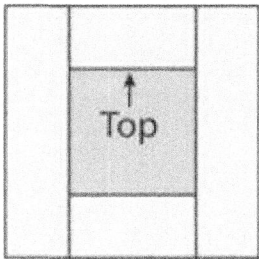

Solid block

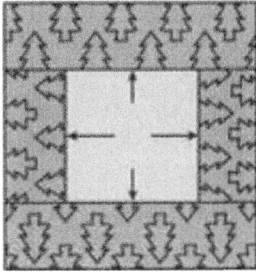

Making the Quilt Top

1. Lay out the finished blocks in 10 rows of 8 blocks as shown in the quilt top assembly diagram. Alternate the blocks between print and solid to form a checkerboard pattern.

2. Sew each row of 8 blocks together. Sew the rows together to finish the quilt top.

Quilt top assembly diagram

Making the Quilt Back

1. Sew 38 of the 2½″ × 10″ strips together, matching the long sides, to create a pieced panel 10″ × 76½″. (Keep in mind that a couple of strips on either end of the panel will end up being cut off when we put the quilt together, so don't put any of your favorites there!

Save the extra strips for another project.)

2. Sew 2½″ × 76½″ neutral solid strips to the top and bottom of the pieced panel. Repeat with the 2 larger print backing pieces, sewing

1 to the top and 1 to the bottom to finish the quilt back.

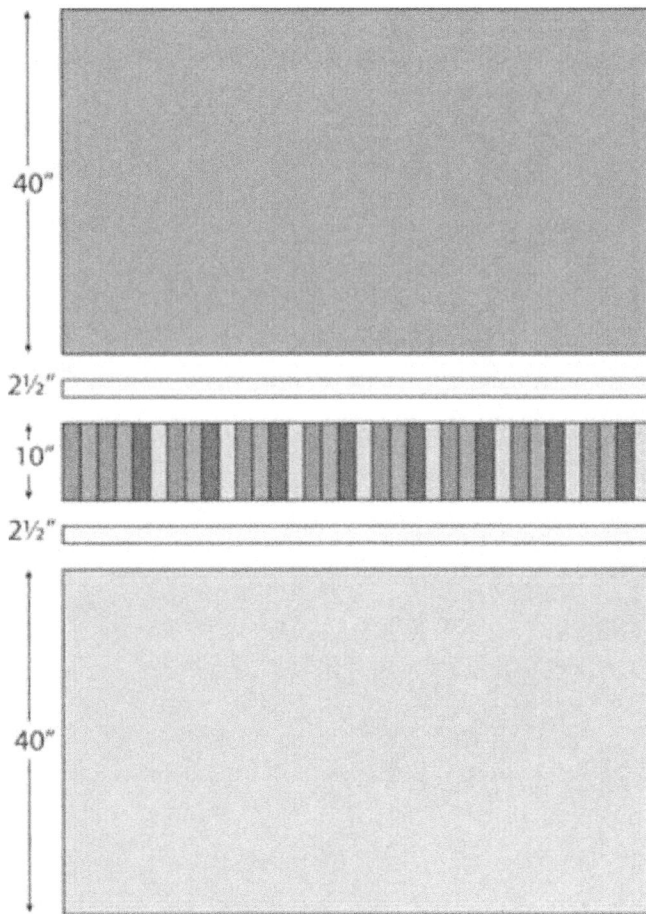

Quit back assembly diagram

Finishing the Quilt

Refer to Step-by-Step Quilt Construction (<u>pages 25</u>–<u>44</u>) for details on sandwiching, quilting, and binding your project.

Alternate Ideas

MAKE IT SIMPLE

Keep the focus on the squares and create a clean, modern composition by substituting all the strips of print fabrics with a second solid fabric.

MAKE IT FUSSY

Cutting the print fabrics to center or otherwise highlight a certain part of the print, commonly called *fussy cutting*, is a particularly effective way to cut the 5″ squares for this pattern. Fussy cutting 80 different 5″ squares from novelty prints can be a great start to an "I Spy" quilt for a child. (For more information, see Fussy Cutting on page 28.)

This sample also dispenses with the solid fabrics entirely, instead using twice as many 2½″ print strips.

More Fabric Options

Use any of the following options as a substitute for the print fabrics used in the quilt blocks:

Option 1: A precut roll of 40 strips 2½″ wide and 2 precut packages of 40 squares 5″ × 5″

• From *each* of the precut 2½″ strips, cut 2 pieces 2½″ × 5″, 2 pieces 2½″ × 9″, and 1 piece 2½″ × 10″.

• Leave the 80 precut 5″ × 5″ squares as they are.

Option 2: ¼ yard each of 40 different fabrics

From *each* of the 40 fabrics, cut:

• 1 strip 2½″ × width of fabric

Subcut *each* strip into 2 pieces 2½″ × 5″, 2 pieces 2½″ × 9″, and 1 piece 2½″ × 10″.

• 1 strip 5″ × width of fabric

Subcut *each* strip into 2 squares 5" × 5".

Option 3: ½ yard each of 10 different fabrics

From *each* of the 10 fabrics, cut:

• 4 strips 2½" × width of fabric

Subcut *each* strip into 2 pieces 2½" × 5", 2 pieces 2½" × 9", and 1 piece 2½" × 10".

• 1 strip 5" × width of fabric

Subcut *each* strip into 8 squares 5" × 5".

Batch of Brownies

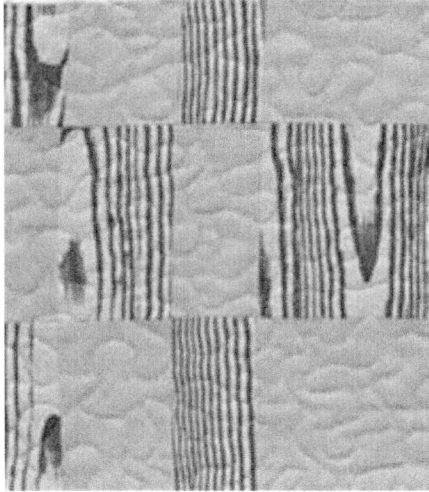

B block

Finished A Block: 8″ × 12″

Finished B Block: 8″ × 9″

Finished C Block: 5″ × 12″

Finished Quilt: 62″ × 62″

Made and machine quilted by Elizabeth Hartman.

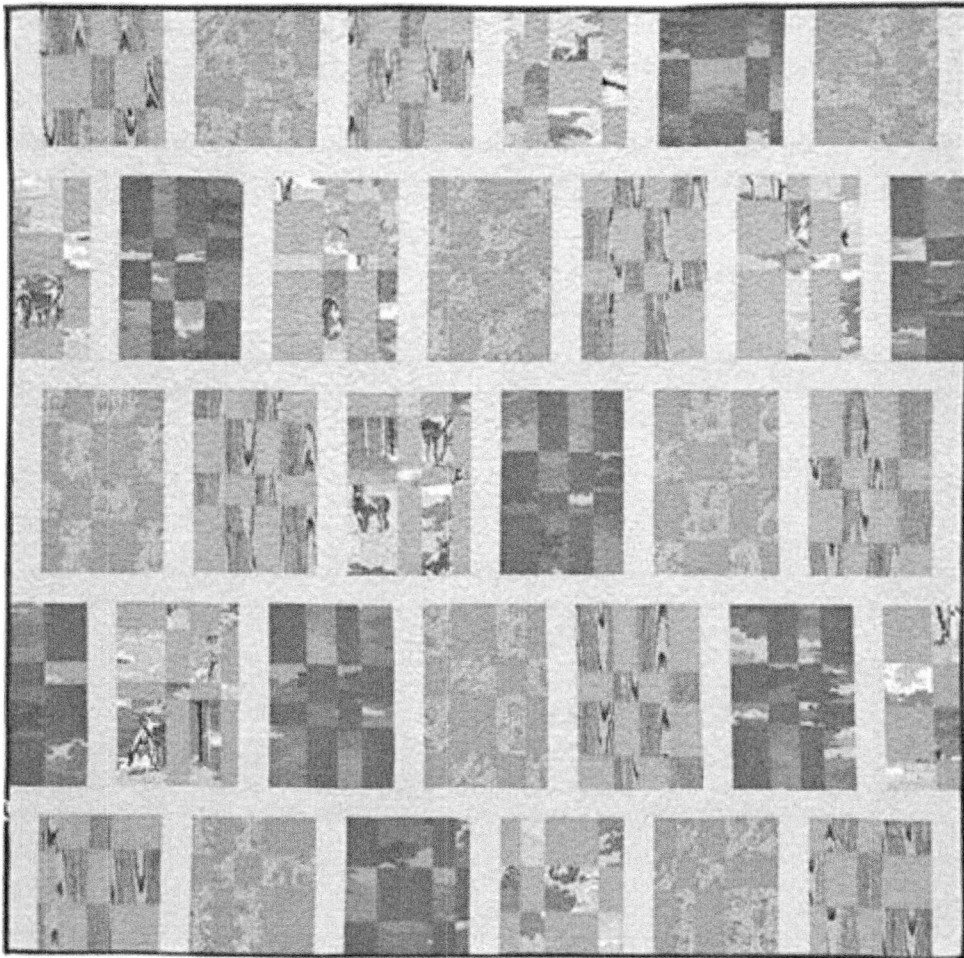

The "stack, cut, and shuffle" method used to make these blocks involves stacking rectangles of fabric and slicing through them in both directions—just like you would a pan of brownies. Once the stacked fabric is sliced, it's then shuffled and sewn back together, creating an abstract checkerboard pattern on each block.

This project also uses an important element of modern quilt design —neutral solid sashing. Adding neutral sashing to a composition gives the eye a "break" among the busier blocks, letting the beautiful print fabrics and vibrant solid fabrics shine.

Don't hesitate to substitute the red, yellow, green, and blue that I used with four different colors of your choice. Regardless of which colors you use, don't get too matchy-matchy with your prints and solids. Choosing a solid that matches one of the less dominant colors in each print will result in a much more interesting look.

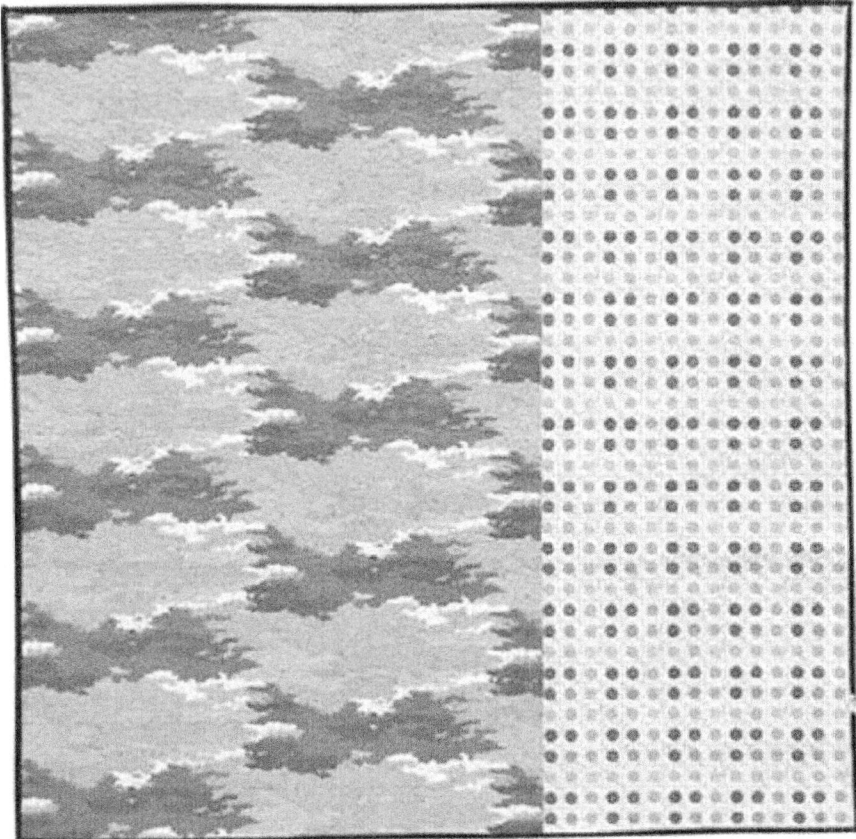

Quilt back

Materials

Yardages are based on fabric that is at least 40" wide, unless otherwise noted.

For the blocks, ½ yard *each* of:

   red print fabric and coordinating solid

   green print fabric and coordinating solid

   yellow print fabric and coordinating solid, at least 42" wide

   blue print fabric and coordinating solid, at least 42" wide

1⅞ yards natural linen or similar neutral solid for sashing

2 yards *each* of 2 different backing fabrics

⅝ yard binding fabric

66" × 66" batting

Cutting Instructions

Red and green coordinating print and solid fabrics:

From *each* ½-yard piece of red and green fabric, cut:

• 1 strip 14½" × width of fabric

Subcut the strip into 3 pieces 10½" × 14½" and 1 piece 6½" × 14½".

Then trim 1 of the 10½" × 14½" pieces to measure 10½" × 11".

From each of these print and solid fabrics, you should have 2 pieces 10½" × 14½", 1 piece 10½" × 11", and 1 piece 6½" × 14½".

Yellow and blue coordinating print and solid fabrics:

From *each* ½-yard piece of yellow and blue fabric, cut:

• 1 strip 14½" × width of fabric

Subcut the strip into 4 pieces 10½" × 14½".

Then trim 2 of these pieces to measure 10½" × 11".

From each of these print and solid fabrics, you should have 2 pieces 10½" × 14½" and 2 pieces 10½" × 11".

Natural linen or similar neutral solid fabric:

For the sashing, unfold the fabric and trim off the selvage edges. Then cut:

• 4 strips 2½" × *length* of fabric

Trim the strips to 63" for horizontal sashing.

• 1 strip 12½" × *length* of fabric

Subcut the strip into 19 pieces 2½" × 12½", for large vertical sashing.

• 1 strip 9½" × *length* of fabric

Subcut the strip into 14 pieces 2½" × 9½", for small vertical sashing.

Backing fabric:

• Trim the selvage edges on *each* of the 2-yard pieces.

Cut 1 of the pieces to measure 30" × *length* of fabric.

Binding fabric:

• Cut 7 strips 2½" × width of fabric.

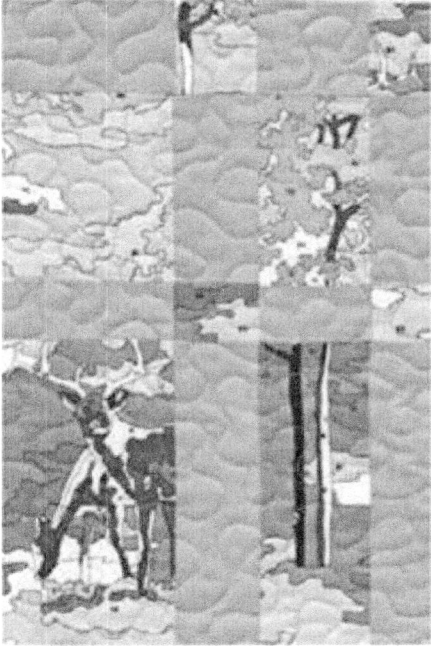

A block

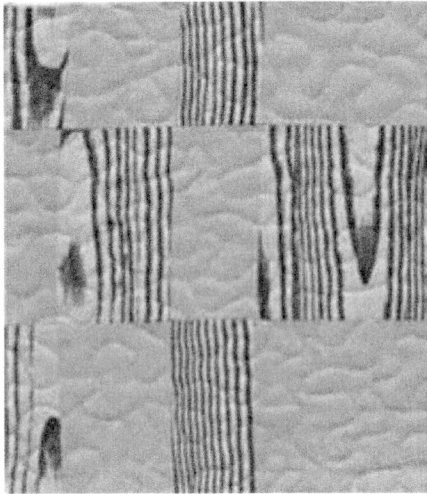

B block

C block

Making the Blocks

All seam allowances are ¼" and all seams are pressed open unless otherwise noted.

Block A

For Block A, use the 10½" × 14½" pieces from each set of print and solid coordinating fabrics. Repeat the following steps to make 4 blocks from *each* set of blue, red, yellow, and green coordinating color sets.

1. Stack the 10½" × 14½" coordinating fabric pieces horizontally in the following order: *print, solid, print, solid*. The edges should line up exactly, and the right sides should face up.

2. Make 3 horizontal cuts through all the layers. The cuts should be spaced randomly but should remain parallel to the sides of the fabric. You should now have 4 stacks of 4 pieces each.

3. On the first and third stacks, move the top print piece to the bottom of the stack.

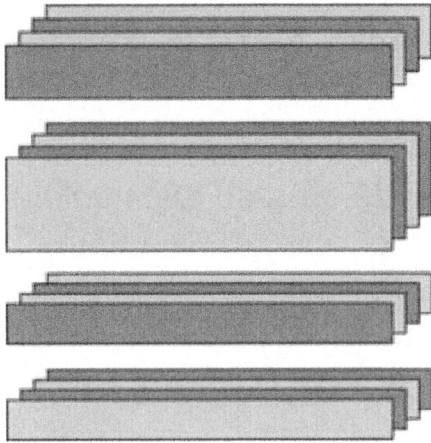

4. Take the top piece from each of the 4 stacks and sew the pieces together along the long edges, right sides together. Repeat the process for the second, third, and fourth stacked layers.

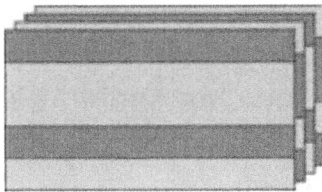

tip

As you cut the stacks of blocks, keep in mind that you'll lose some size to seam allowances when the blocks are sewn back together. To maintain a uniform look among the blocks, I recommend cutting each horizontal section a minimum of 1½" wide.

5. Stack the pieced units with seams running vertically, making sure that the seams match, the edges are lined up, and the fabric in the top left corner is stacked as follows: *solid, print, solid, print.*

6. Make 3 horizontal cuts through all the layers. You should have 4 stacks of 4 pieced units each.

7. On the first and third stacks, move the top unit to the bottom of the stack. Each layer of stacks should now be able to fit together in an abstract checkerboard pattern.

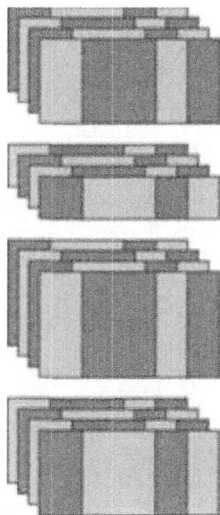

8. Take the top unit from each of the 4 stacks and sew the 4 units together, with right sides facing and seams matching. Repeat for the other 3 layers.

9. Trim each of the 4 blocks to a perfect 8½″ × 12½″.

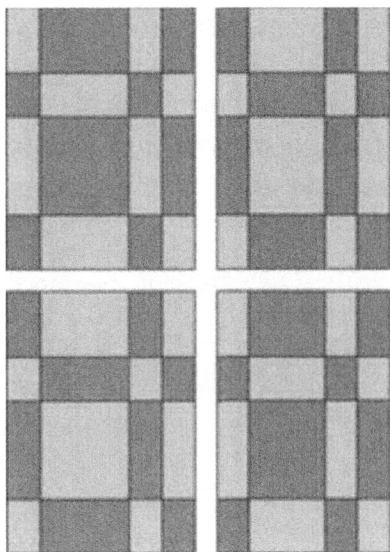

You should now have a total of 16 Block A's: 4 each of blue, red, yellow, and green.

Block B

For Block B, use the 10½″ × 11″ pieces from each set of print and solid coordinating fabrics. Repeat the following steps with the coordinating color sets to make 4 blocks from each set of blue and yellow, and 2 blocks from green and red.

1. Stack, cut, and sew together the 10½″ × 11″ coordinating fabric pieces as for Block A, Steps 1–5.

2. Make 2 horizontal cuts through all the layers. The cuts should be spaced randomly but should remain parallel to the sides of the fabric. When cutting the blue and yellow units, you should have 3 stacks of 4 pieced units each. When cutting the green and red units, you should have 3 stacks of 2 pieced units each.

138

3. On the first and third stacks, move the top unit to the bottom of the stack. Each layer of the stacks should now be able to fit together in an abstract checkerboard pattern.

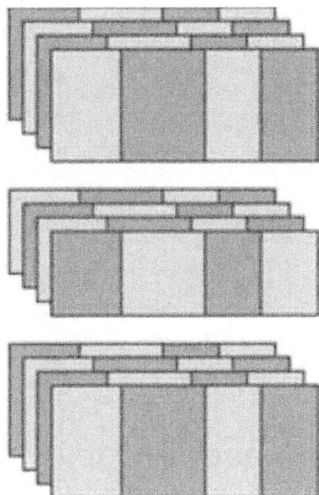

4. Take the top unit from each of the 3 stacks and sew the 3 units together, with right sides facing and seams matching. Repeat for the other layers.

5. Trim each of the blocks to a perfect 8½″ × 9½″.

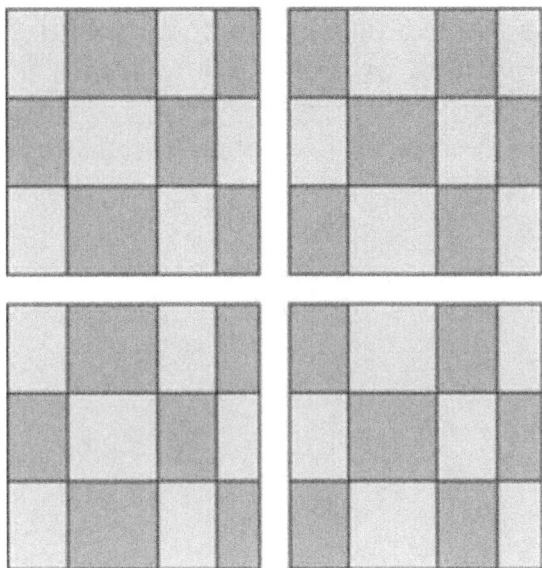

You should now have a total of 12 Block B's: 4 each of blue and yellow and 2 each of green and red.

Block C

For Block C, use the 6½" × 14½" pieces from the green and red coordinating fabrics. Repeat the following steps to make 2 blocks from each green and red color set.

1. Stack the 6½" × 14½" coordinating fabric pieces horizontally in the following order: *print, solid.* The edges should line up exactly, and the right sides should be facing up.

2. Make 1 horizontal cut through both layers. The cut should remain parallel to the sides of the fabric. You should now have 2 stacks of 2 pieces each.

3. Move the top print piece of the first stack to the bottom of the stack.

4. Take the top piece from each stack and sew the 2 pieces together along the long edges, right sides together. Repeat to sew the 2 pieces in the bottom layer together.

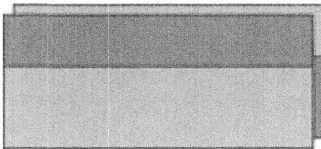

5. Stack the 2 pieced units with the seams running vertically, making sure that the seams match and the edges are lined up.

6. Make 3 horizontal cuts through both layers. You should have 4 stacks of 2 pieced units each.

7. On the first and third stacks, move the top unit to the bottom of the stack. Each layer of the stacks should now be able to fit together in an abstract checkerboard pattern.

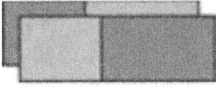

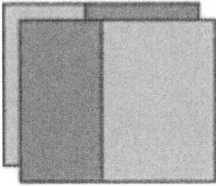

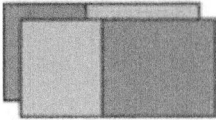

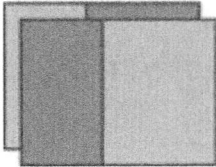

8. Take the top unit from each of the 4 stacks and sew the 4 units together, with right sides facing and seams matching. Repeat for the second layer of pieces.

9. Trim the 2 blocks to a perfect 5½″ × 12½″.

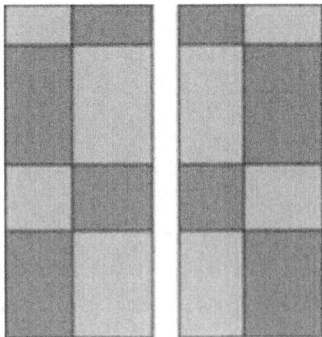

You should now have a total of 4 Block C's: 2 each of green and red.

Making the Quilt Top

1. Sew 5 rows of blocks as shown in the quilt top assembly diagram. Alternate the placement of colored blocks within each row. Place the small vertical sashing between each Block B, and the large vertical sashing between each Block A and Block C.

2. Sew the 5 rows and 4 horizontal sashing pieces together as shown in the quilt top assembly diagram. Trim the horizontal sashing even with the sides of the quilt top.

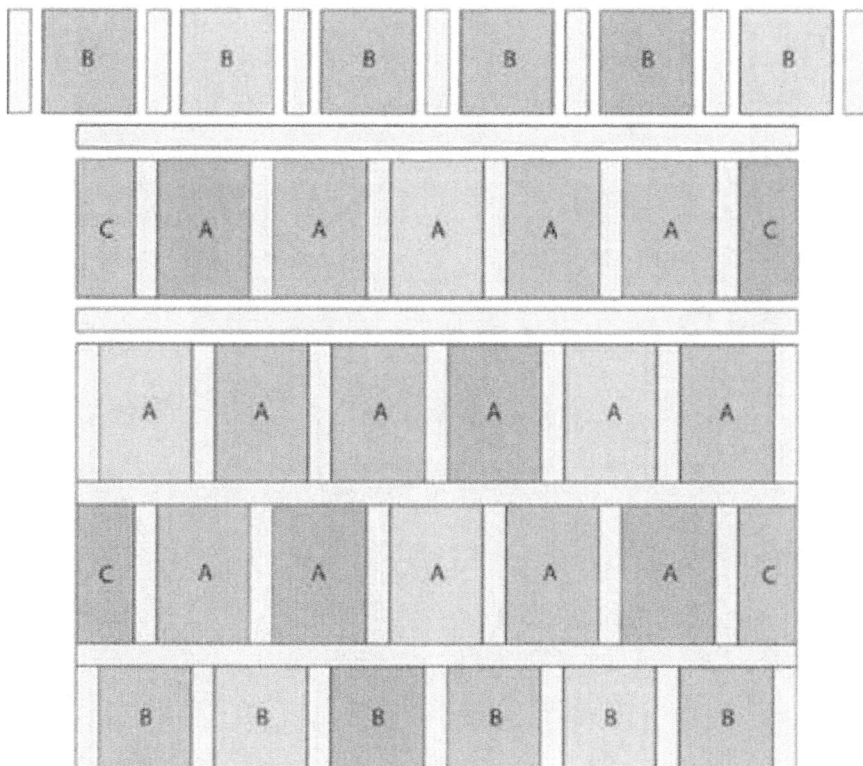

Quilt top assembly diagram

Making the Quilt Back

Sew the 30"-wide backing fabric, along the long (72") side, to the uncut backing fabric.

Finishing the Quilt

Refer to Step-by-Step Quilt Construction (pages 25–44) for details on sandwiching, quilting, and binding your project.

Alternate Ideas

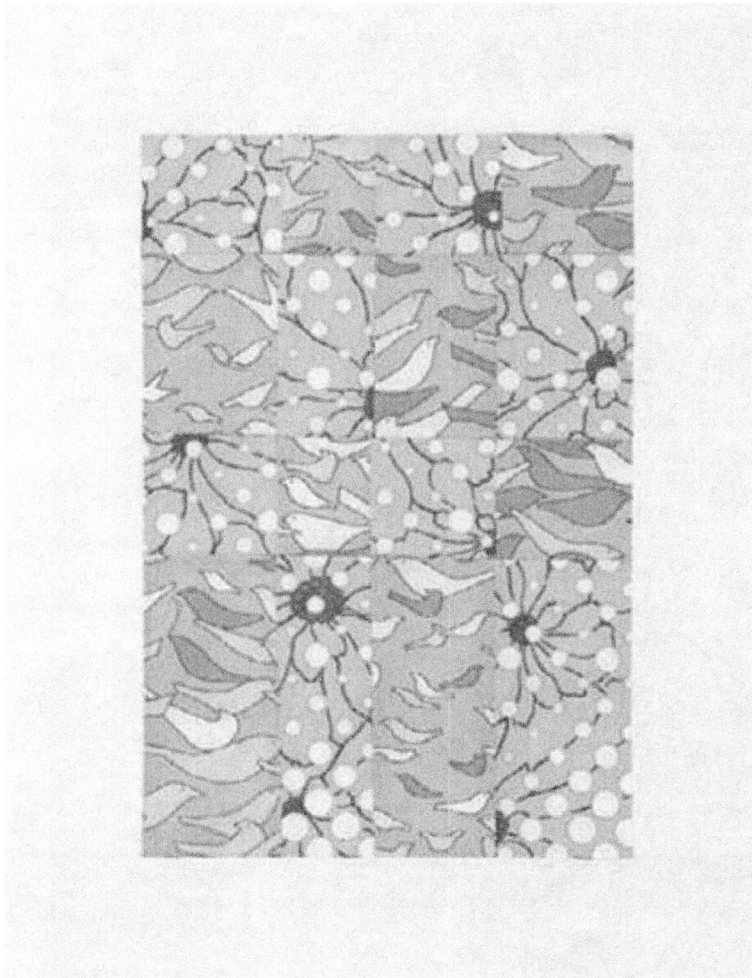

MAKE IT SCRAPPY

You can easily use the same basic layout and block construction method without using the color-coding system described in the pattern. To make this quilt, you need 16 of Block A, which can be made from 16 pieces 10½" × 14½"; 12 of Block B, which can be made from 12 pieces 10½" × 11"; and 4 of Block C, which can be made from 4 pieces 6½" × 14½".

MAKE IT WITH LARGE AND SMALL PRINTS

Instead of using solids, pair a large and small print in each of the 4 colors. This can be an especially effective way to use 8 fabrics from the same collection.

Projects for the Confident Beginner

Kitchen Window by Elizabeth Hartman (see page 77)

Valentine

Quilt block

Finished Block: 10½″ × 10½″

Finished Quilt: 63″ × 84″

Made and machine quilted by Elizabeth Hartman.

Materials

Yardages are based on fabric that is at least 40" wide, unless otherwise noted.

Variety of fabric strips, for blocks

You will need a total of 8–10 yards of fabric that is cut into strips measuring 1"–2½" wide × 3"–16" long. Select a variety of print and solid fabric strips in 4 color groups. Your composition will be more interesting if you include more than 1 color in some of the groups and some of the print fabrics. I used prints and solids in the following color groups: reds and violets; gold, orange, and pink; greenish blues; and yellowish greens.

Note: The amount of fabric you will need depends on how many strips you use and how wide they are. Using fewer but wider strips on each block will generally take less fabric than using many thinner strips.

1 yard neutral solid fabric, for sashing

⅜ yard *each* of 3 coordinating solid fabrics, for backing

2 yards *each* of 2 coordinating print fabrics, at least 42" wide, for backing

¾ yard binding fabric

67" × 88" batting

48 sheets 11" × 17" copier paper, trimmed to 11" square

Washable gluestick

Quilts like this one that are made with hundreds of narrow fabric strips are commonly called string quilts. Because it can be tricky to stabilize so many thin strips of fabric, string quilts often use a technique called foundation piecing.

Foundation piecing uses a secondary material, in this case plain old copier paper, as a base onto which the patchwork strips are pieced. Using a smaller-than-normal stitch length on the machine perforates the paper as the strips are sewn, making it easy to tear the paper away once each block is complete.

For this quilt, divide your fabric strips into four color groups to create a striking color-coded diamond pattern.

Quilt back

Cutting Instructions

Variety of fabric strips:
See Materials for cutting instructions.

Neutral solid fabric:
For the sashing, cut:

- 2 strips 16" × width of fabric

Subcut these strips into 48 sashing strips 1½" × 16".

Backing fabric:

From *each* solid backing fabric, trim away the selvages and cut:

- 2 strips 4½" × width of fabric

From *each* print backing fabric, trim away the selvages and cut:

- 1 strip 18½" × *length* of fabric
- 1 strip 22½" × *length* of fabric

Binding fabric:

- Cut 8 strips 2½" × width of fabric.

tip

If you're cutting the fabric strips from new yardage instead of from scraps, cut strips 1"–2½" × width of fabric. As you piece your blocks, you can cut the exact strip length you need from these longer strips.

Making the Blocks

All seam allowances are ¼", and all seams are pressed open unless otherwise noted.

1. Assign each of the color groups a number, 1 through 4, and place each group of strips in a separate plastic bin or other accessible container.

2. Use a long quilting ruler (18"–24") and a pencil to draw a diagonal line between opposite corners of an 11" × 11" square of copier paper. Draw a parallel line ¾" from each side of the line you just drew, creating a 1½"-wide diagonal stripe that runs through the center of the paper.

3. Use a gluestick to place a small amount of glue along the center of this stripe, taking care to keep glue away from the edges where you'll be sewing. Center a 1½" × 16" sashing strip on the stripe, pressing down to make sure it sticks to the glue. (Don't worry about the glue on the fabric. After the fabric takes a trip through the washer, you'll never know the glue was there.)

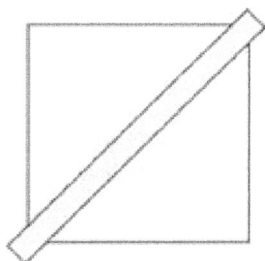

4. Place a strip of fabric from Color Group 1 on top of one side of the sashing strip, lining up the edges and placing the right sides together as shown. Sew the 2 pieces together through all the layers, including the paper, using a standard ¼" seam allowance but a smaller than usual stitch length (see the Tip on page 74).

5. Press the strip toward the outside of the block.

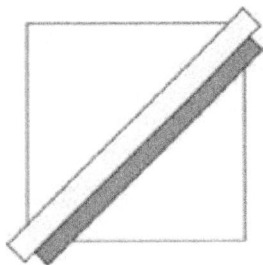

6. Using the same method described in Steps 4 and 5, keep adding strips from Color Group 1 until all the paper on one side of the block is covered. Use the same method and strips from Color Group 2 to cover the other half of the block.

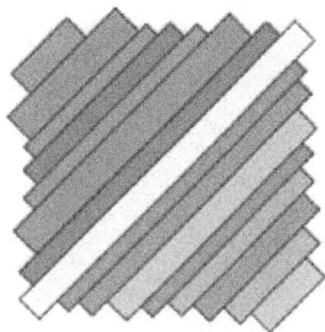

7. Turn the block over and use the paper as a guide to trim the block to a perfect 11″ × 11″ square.

8. Repeat Steps 2–7 to make 11 more blocks (12 total) that are pieced with strips from Color Group 1 on one side and Color Group 2 on the other.

9. Make 12 blocks that are pieced with strips from Color Group 2 on one side and Color Group 3 on the other.

10. Make 12 blocks that are pieced with strips from Color Group 3 on one side and Color Group 4 on the other.

11. Make 12 blocks that are pieced with strips from Color Group 4 on one side and Color Group 1 on the other.

Group 1/2

Group 2/3

Group 3/4

Group 4/1

12. Carefully tear the paper backing away from all the blocks.

Making the Quilt Top

1. Arrange the finished blocks in 8 rows of 6 blocks as shown in the quilt top assembly diagram, matching like-colored block halves to form larger like-colored diamonds. The neutral sashing running through the center of each block should match up to form a lattice pattern across the top of the quilt.

2. Sew the blocks into rows, and sew the rows together to complete the quilt top.

Quilt top assembly diagram

tip
The fabric along the edges of the blocks will have been cut on the bias, which means it will be prone to stretching. Keep this in mind and be especially careful when pinning and sewing the blocks together.

Making the Quilt Back

1. Sew each pair of like solid 4½″ strips together, end to end. Trim each to 72″.

2. Sew together the pieced solid strips and the wider print strips as shown in the quilt back assembly diagram.

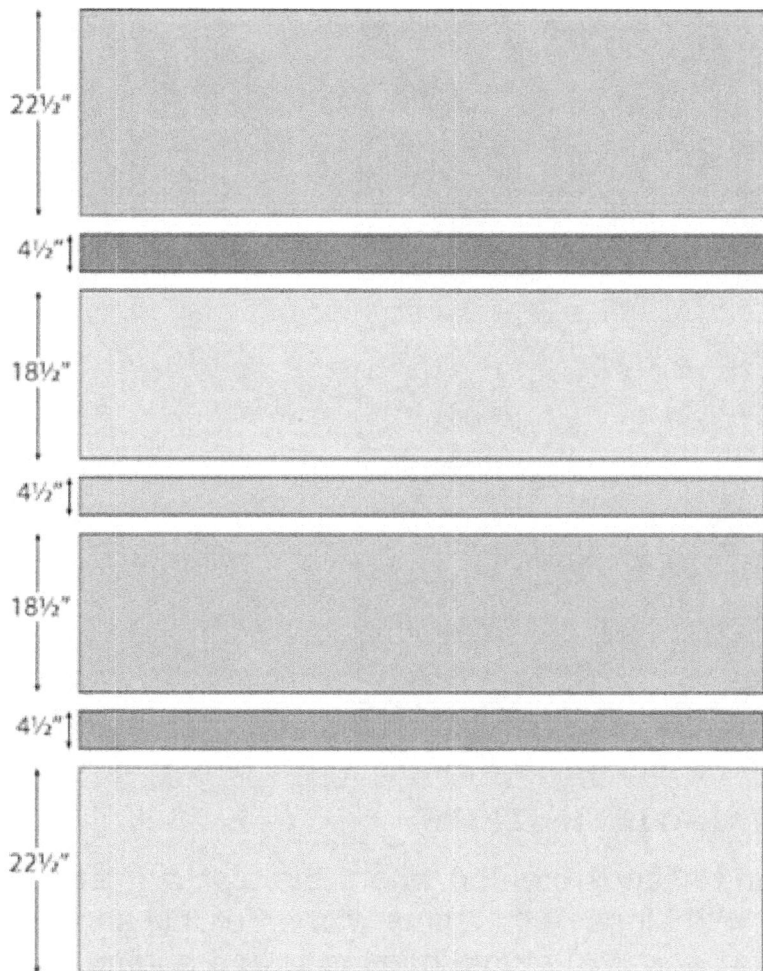

Quilt back assembly diagram

Finishing the Quilt

Refer to Step-by-Step Quilt Construction (pages 25–44) for details on sandwiching, quilting, and binding your project.

Alternate Ideas

MAKE IT WITH EQUAL-WIDTH STRIPS

Emphasize the diamond shapes created where the blocks intersect by piecing each block with strips of the same width. For this sample, I alternated piecing 1½″ and 2½″ strips, beginning and ending with 1½″ strips. Piecing an entire quilt this way will create bold diamond shapes that look a lot like Square-in-Square blocks with mitered corners.

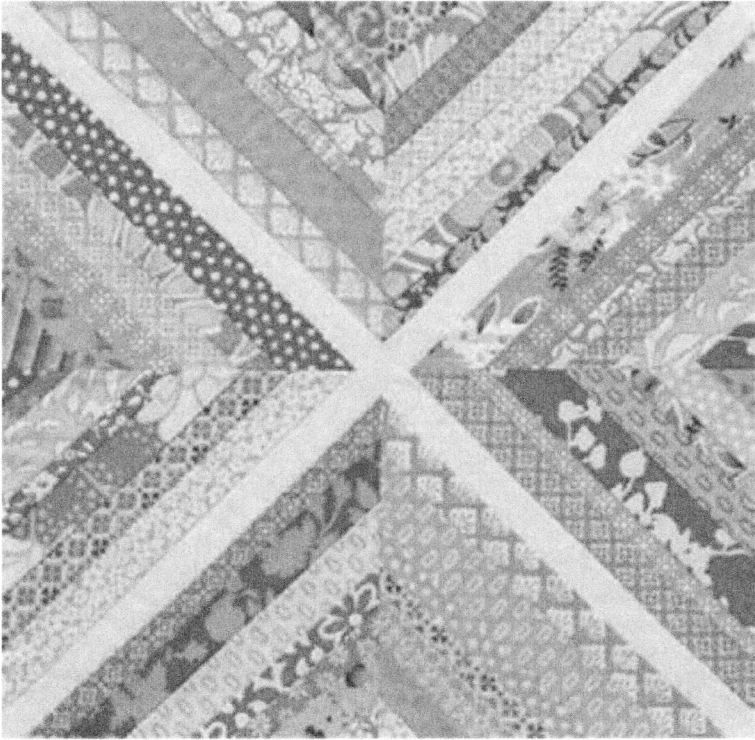

MAKE IT SCRAPPY

Instead of dividing the strips by color, place them randomly for a scrappy look. This block uses some of the same fabrics as the color-coded quilt.

Kitchen Window

Finished Block: 16″ × 16″

Finished Quilt: 52″ × 68″

Made and machine quilted by Elizabeth Hartman.

Materials

Yardages are based on fabric that is at least 40" wide, unless otherwise noted.

12 different 12" × 16" pieces of print fabrics[*] for quilt blocks

1⅝ yards dark solid fabric for block window frames

2 yards neutral solid fabric for quilt borders and sashing

1¾ yards *each* of 1 large-print and 1 small-print coordinating fabrics for backing

⅝ yard binding fabric

56" × 72" batting

12 organizer cards

See More Fabric Options (page 81) for alternate fabric and cutting instructions.

Have you ever wanted to frame an especially lovely print fabric? Here's a way to do it in the context of a quilt. Each block is pieced to look like an abstract window frame. Use the spaces in each frame to highlight your favorite print fabrics.

Quilt back

Cutting Instructions

Quilt block print fabrics:

Note: As you cut, stack pieces of corresponding size together.

From *each* of the 12″ × 16″ print fabrics, cut:

- 1 strip 6″ × 16″

Subcut this strip into 1 window piece 6″ × 6½″ and 2 window pieces 6″ × 3½″.

- 1 strip 4″ × 16″

Subcut this strip into 1 window piece 4″ × 8½″ and 1 window piece 4″ × 5½″.

You should now have the following cut from the print fabric for the block construction:

- 12 window pieces 6″ × 6½″

- 24 window pieces 6″ × 3½″

- 12 window pieces 4″ × 8½″

- 12 window pieces 4″ × 5½″

Dark solid fabric:

For the block window frames, cut:

- 1 strip 6″ × width of fabric

Subcut this strip into 24 window frame pieces 1½″ × 6″.

Dark solid fabric continued:

- 1 strip 4″ × width of fabric

Subcut this strip into 12 window frame pieces 1½″ × 4″.

- 2 strips 14½″ × width of fabric

Subcut the strips into 36 vertical window frame pieces 1½″ × 14½″.

- 1 strip 12½″ × width of fabric

Subcut this strip into 24 horizontal window frame pieces 1½″ × 12½″.

Neutral solid fabric:

For the quilt sashing and borders, trim the selvage edges and cut:

- 4 border strips 2½" × *length* of fabric

- 1 strip 16½" × *length* of fabric

  Subcut this strip into 24 sashing pieces 2½" × 16½".

Backing fabrics:

- Trim the selvage edges on *each* fabric and cut to measure 60" long.

- Cut the coordinating small-print backing fabric into 2 pieces measuring 18" × 60".

Binding fabric:

- Cut 7 strips 2½" × width of fabric.

Making the Blocks

All seam allowances are ¼", and all seams are pressed open unless otherwise noted.

Sorting the pieces

On a large table or other open area, lay out 12 organizer cards. Sort the cut pieces among the cards, adding the following to each:

- 2 window pieces 6" × 3½"

- 1 window piece 6" × 6½"

- 1 window piece 4" × 5½"

- 1 window piece 4" × 8½"

- 2 small window frame pieces 1½" × 6"

- 1 small window frame piece 1½" × 4"

- 3 vertical window frame pieces 1½" × 14½"

- 2 horizontal window frame pieces 1½" × 12½"

- 2 side sashing pieces 2½" × 16½"

Stack the organizer cards and use the following instructions to sew 1 block from each of the 12 cards for a total of 12 blocks.

Sewing the blocks

1. Make a pieced column 6" × 14½" by sewing together window and frame pieces as shown.

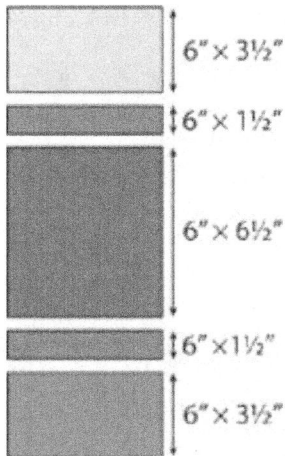

6" × 3½"

6" × 1½"

6" × 6½"

6" × 1½"

6" × 3½"

2. Make another pieced column 4" × 14½" by sewing together window and frame pieces as shown.

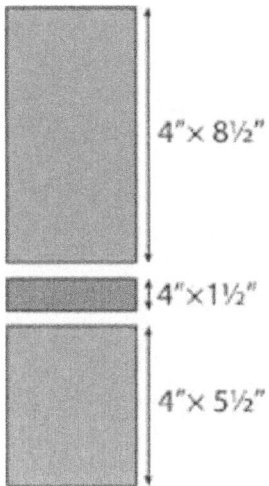

4" × 8½"

4" × 1½"

4" × 5½"

3. Sew together pieced columns and 1½" × 14½" vertical window frame pieces as shown.

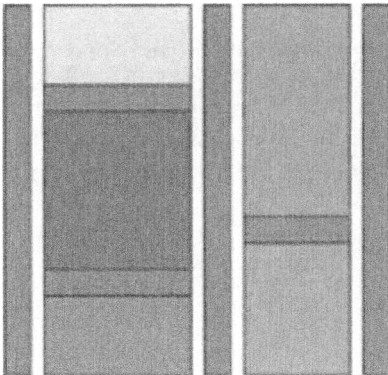

4. Sew 1½" × 12½" horizontal window frame pieces to the top and bottom of the block.

5. Finish the block by sewing a 2½" × 16½" side sashing piece to each side.

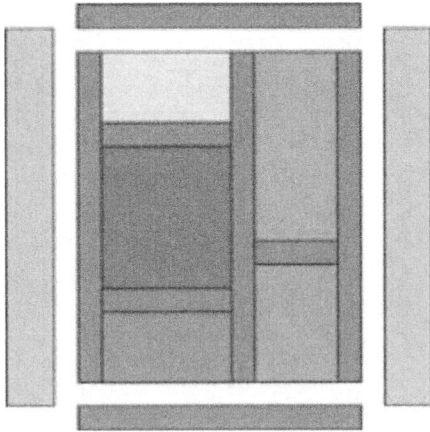

Making the Quilt Top

1. Sew the finished blocks into 4 rows of 3 blocks each, rotating every other block 90°. Sew the rows together.

2. Sew 1 border strip to the left side and 1 to the right side of the quilt top and trim the excess border strip fabric. Sew the remaining border strips to the top and bottom to complete the quilt top. Trim excess length from the borders at the corners to create a perfect rectangle 52½″ × 68½″.

Quilt top assembly diagram

Making the Quilt Back

Join an 18" × 60" small-print backing fabric piece to each side of the large-print backing fabric, matching the edges along the long (60") sides.

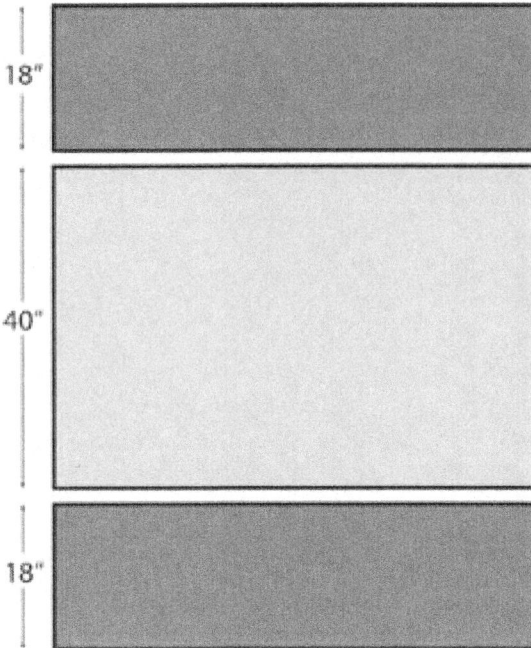

Quilt back assembly diagram

Finishing the Quilt

Refer to Step-by-Step Quilt Construction (<u>pages 25</u>–<u>44</u>) for details on sandwiching, quilting, and binding your project.

Alternate Ideas

MAKE IT FUSSY

The concepts of frames and looking through windows work wonderfully with fussy-cut print fabrics. For a quilt this size, you'll need 12 window pieces each in the following sizes: 6" × 6½", 4" × 5½", and 4" × 8½". You'll also need 24 window pieces 6" × 3½". (See page 28 for more information on fussy cutting.) Remember, you'll be rotating every other block, so be aware when positioning directional fabrics.

MAKE IT CRAZY

Of course those window frames don't have to be filled with a single piece of fabric. Randomly pieced fabric cut down to size can make a big impact!

More Fabric Options

Use the following option as a substitute for the print fabrics used in the quilt blocks:

6 different fat quarters of print fabrics

Note: As you cut, stack pieces of corresponding size together.

From *each* fat quarter, cut:

• 1 strip 6″ × *length* of fat quarter (approximately 21″)

Subcut this strip into 2 window pieces 6″ × 6½″ and 2 window pieces 6″ × 3½″.

• 1 strip 4″ × *length* of fat quarter

Subcut this strip into 2 window pieces 4″ × 8½″.

• From the remaining fabric in each fat quarter, cut 2 window pieces 6″ × 3½″ and 2 window pieces 4″ × 5½″.

Planetarium

Quilt block

Finished Block: 14½″ × 14½″

Finished Quilt: 68″ × 68″

Made and machine quilted by Elizabeth Hartman.

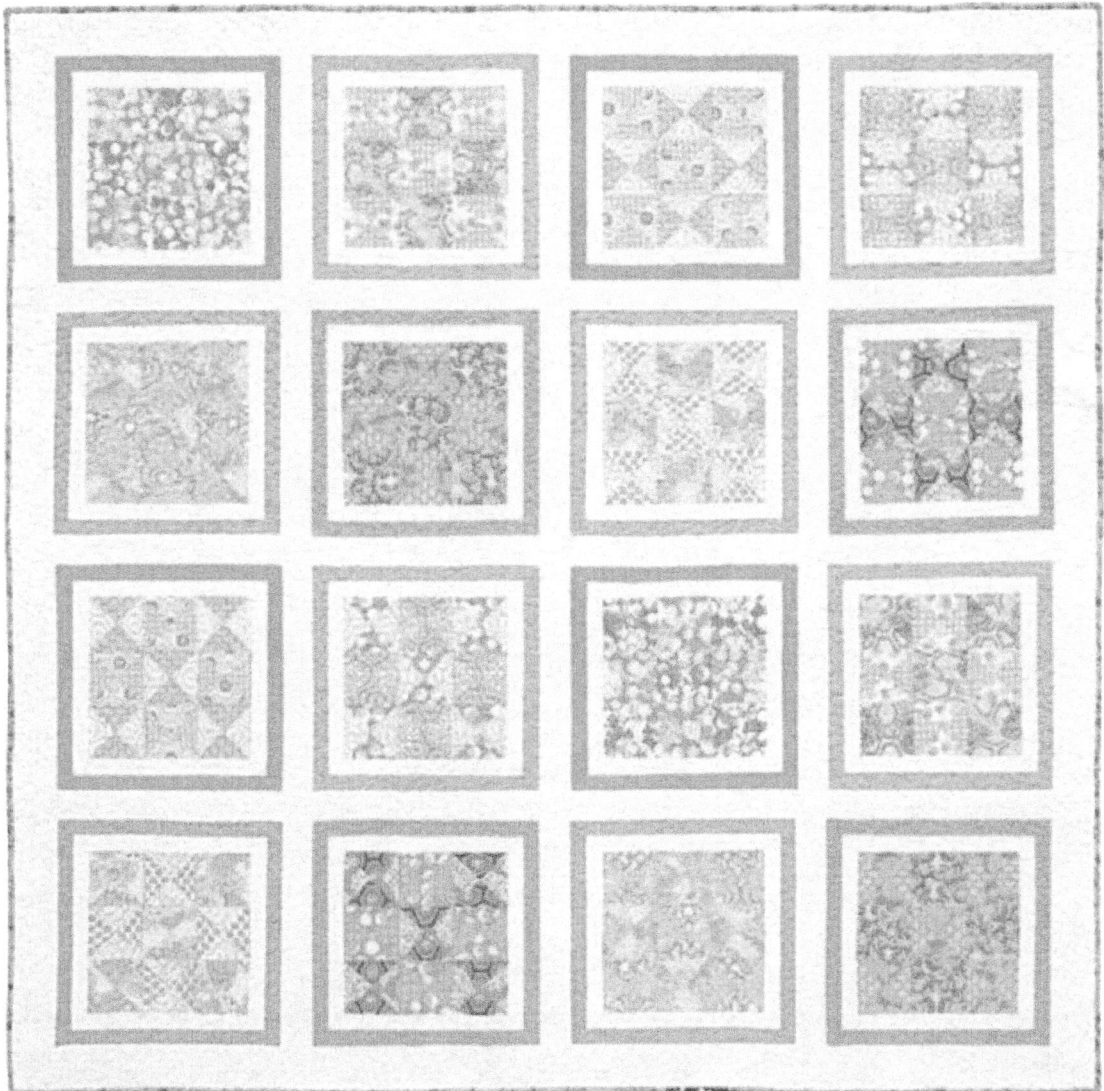

In general, warm colors such as red, orange, and yellow advance or appear dominant in a composition. Cool colors such as green, blue, and violet recede or appear less dominant. This quilt plays with the contrast between the two groups of colors.

The blocks feature smaller traditional Hourglass blocks as components. The Hourglass units are made using quarter-square triangles, which is a fancy way of describing the process of cutting a square into four triangles by making two diagonal cuts from corner to corner.

Quilt back

Materials

Yardages are based on fabric that is at least 40" wide, unless otherwise noted.

80 warm-colored 5″ × 5″ print fabric squares* for Hourglass units

80 cool-colored 5″ × 5″ print fabric squares* for Hourglass units

½ yard *each* of 2 warm-colored and 2 cool-colored coordinating solid fabrics for block frames

3¼ yards neutral solid fabric for block frames, sashing, and quilt back

2¼ yards *each* of 1 warm-colored and 1 cool-colored print fabric for backing

⅝ yard binding fabric

72″ × 72″ batting

See Precut Squares (page 10) for options on cutting 5″ × 5″ squares.

Cutting Instructions

5″ × 5″ squares:

- Cut the 80 squares into quarter-square triangles, see Making the Blocks (at right).

Coordinating solid fabrics:

From each of the ½-yard solid fabrics, cut:

- 8 strips 1½″ × width of fabric

Subcut *each* strip into 1 piece 1½" × 13" and 1 piece 1½" × 15" for the block frames.

Neutral solid fabric:[*]

From the 3 yards of fabric, cut in the following order:

- 11 strips 1½" × width of fabric

Subcut the strips into a total of 32 pieces 1½" × 11", for the block inner frame.

- 11 strips 1½" × width of fabric

Subcut the strips into a total of 32 pieces 1½" × 13", for the block inner frame.

- 10 strips 2½" × *length* of remaining fabric

Save 5 of these strips as long sashing for the quilt top.

From the other 5 strips, cut 20 short sashing pieces 2½" × 14½" for the quilt top.

- 2 strips 1½" × *length* of remaining fabric, for the quilt back

- From the remaining fabric, cut 15 pieces 1½" × 4" and 2 pieces 3" × 4", for the quilt back.

Backing fabric:

- Trim off the selvage edges and trim *each* fabric to measure 36" × 76".

Binding fabric:

- Cut 8 strips 2½" × width of fabric.

[*]*This pattern uses a number of different sashing pieces that may not be easy to tell apart unless they're labeled. As you cut the neutral*

solid fabric, put a label or sticky note with measurements on each stack of same-sized pieces.

Making the Blocks

All seam allowances are ¼", and all seams are pressed open unless otherwise noted.

Making the Hourglass units

1. Cut each of the 80 warm-colored precut 5″ × 5″ squares diagonally from corner to corner into 4 quarter-square triangles as shown.

2. Sort the quarter-square triangles into 80 sets of 4. Each set should have 2 triangles each of 2 different warm-colored print fabrics.

3. For each of the 80 sets, sew 1 triangle of each print together along the bias-cut edge, creating 2 larger pieced triangles. Sew the 2 pieced triangles together, matching the center seams.

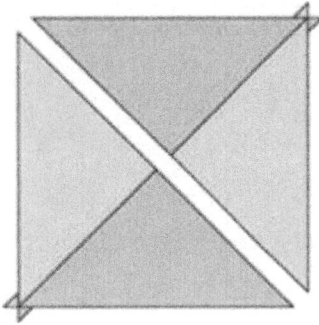

tip

Fabric cut on the bias, such as the short edges of the quarter-square triangles used in this project, is prone to stretching. Take your time sewing the triangles, using plenty of pins to keep the seams straight.

4. Measuring 2″ from the center on all sides, trim each of the 80 warm-colored Hourglass units to a perfect 4″ × 4″ square.

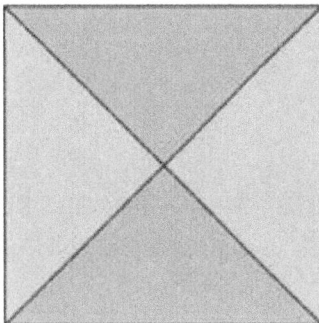

5. Repeat Steps 1–4 with the 80 cool-colored 5″ squares to make 80 cool-colored Hourglass units.

6. Set aside 8 warm-colored and 8 cool-colored Hourglass units to use on the quilt back.

1. Divide the remaining 144 Hourglass units into 8 sets of 9 warm-colored units and 8 sets of 9 cool-colored units. Sew each set of 9 into 3 rows of 3, and sew the 3 rows together. The 16 completed nine-patch units are the centers of the large quilt blocks.

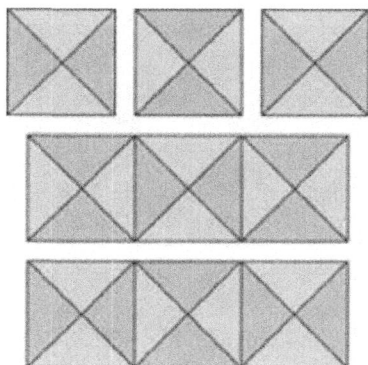

2. Sew 1½" × 11" neutral solid strips to the top and bottom of each nine-patch unit. Then sew a 1½" × 13" strip to each side, creating a frame around the Hourglass nine-patch.

3. Divide the framed nine-patch units into 2 sets of 4 warm-colored units and 2 sets of 4 cool-colored units.

4. Sort the coordinating solid 1½" × 13" and 1½" × 15" pieces among the nine-patch sets. For each set, you'll use a different-colored solid fabric for the outer frame. Match warm solids with warm blocks and cool solids with cool blocks.

5. Sew a 1½" × 13" coordinating solid to the top and bottom of each nine-patch set. Then sew a 1½" × 15" coordinating solid to each side, creating an outer frame around each of the 16 blocks.

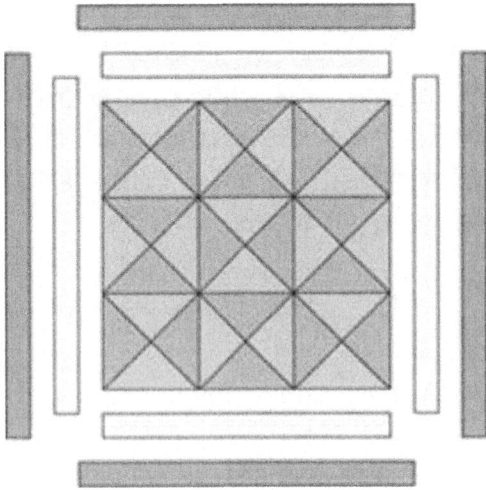

tip

Keep your piecing accurate by squaring up the blocks after sewing each solid frame.

Making the Quilt Top

1. Arrange the blocks in 4 rows of 4, alternating warm-colored and cool-colored blocks. Sew together each row, adding short sashing pieces between blocks and on both ends of each row.

2. Sew together the pieced rows as shown in the quilt top assembly diagram, sewing long sashing strips between rows, as well as to the top and bottom of the quilt top. Trim excess sashing length from the sides to create a 68½" × 68½" square quilt top.

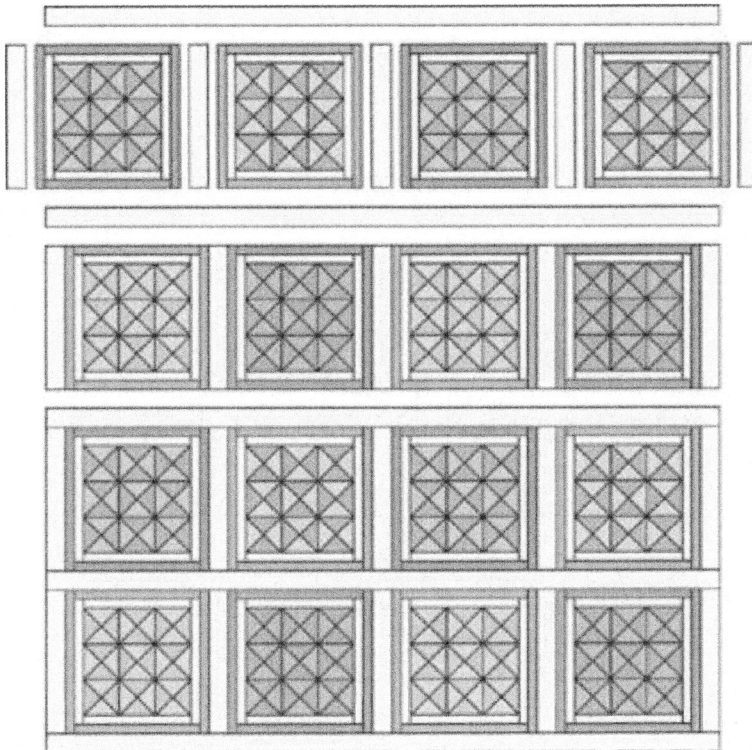

Quilt top assembly diagram

Making the Quilt Back

1. Piece a row of 16 Hourglass units, alternating warm and cool blocks, and sewing 1½" × 4" neutral solid pieces between units as shown in the quilt back assembly diagram.

2. Sew a 3" × 4" neutral solid piece to each end of the pieced Hourglass panel. Sew the long 1½" neutral solid strips to each long side of the pieced panel, trimming excess length as necessary.

3. Sew 1 of the backing pieces to one side of the pieced panel and the other to the other side to complete the quilt back.

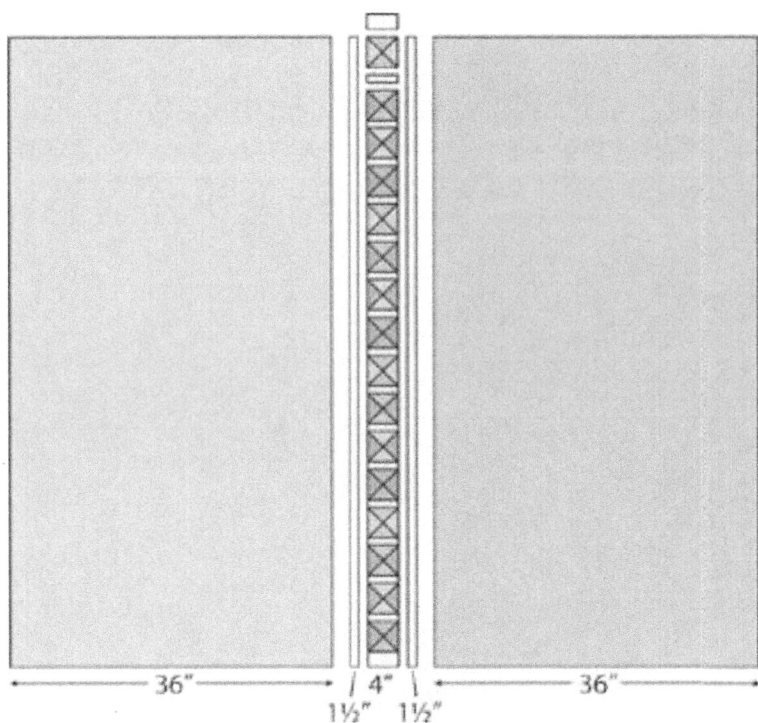

Quilt back assembly diagram

Finishing the Quilt

Refer to Step-by-Step Quilt Construction (pages 25–44) for details on sandwiching, quilting, and binding your project.

Alternate Ideas

MAKE IT SIMPLE

Skip dividing the prints into warm and cool groups and emphasize the pieced triangles by making half of each Hourglass unit from the neutral solid. For a quilt this size, use 80 squares cut from assorted print fabrics and 80 squares cut from the neutral solid. (You'll need an additional 1½ yards of the neutral solid fabric for this.)

Choose coordinating solid fabrics in your 4 favorite colors from the print fabrics you're using.

MAKE IT WITH TWO COLORS

This pattern also works well with different monochromatic prints in 2 colors. Use 80 squares cut from print fabrics in each of the 2 colors to make the 160 Hourglass units. (Each Hourglass unit will use 2 triangles of each color.)

Instead of using ½ yard each of 4 coordinating solids, use ⅞ yard each of solid fabrics in your 2 colors. Cut 16 of each coordinating block frame piece from each of the 2 colors, which will be enough to put one color solid frame on half of the blocks and the other color on the other half of the blocks.

Little Leaves

Quilt block

Finished Block: 12″ × 12″

Finished Quilt: 48″ × 48″

Made and machine quilted by Elizabeth Hartman.

This quilt's simple leaf-shaped appliqués are easy to machine stitch, but they create a lovely, complex pattern when the finished blocks are sewn together. Lightweight fusible web is used to hold the "leaves" in place, while buttonhole or satin stitching secures them permanently.

This quilt will be most successful when there is a lot of contrast between the print fabrics of the appliqués and the neutral solid blocks.

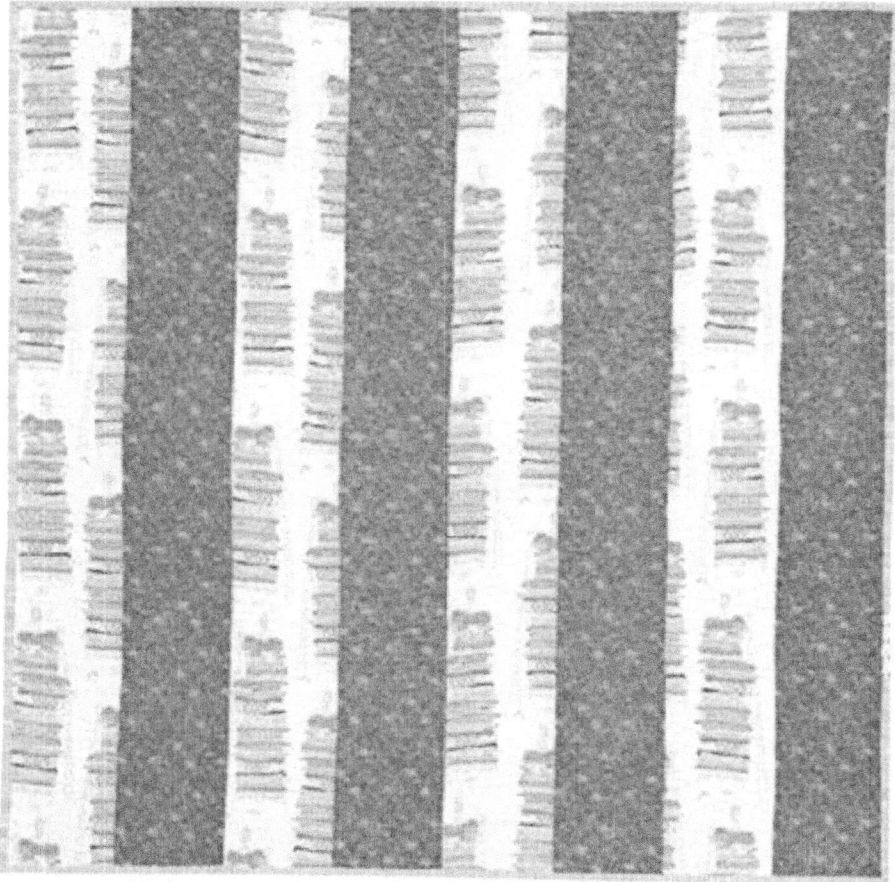

Quilt back

Materials

Yardages are based on fabric that is at least 40" wide, unless otherwise noted.

16 different print fabric scraps*, approximately 10″ × 10″ each for leaf appliqués

2¼ yards white or light-colored neutral solid for block background

1¾ yards *each* of 2 different print fabrics for backing

½ yard binding fabric

52″ × 52″ batting

4¼ yards 17″-wide lightweight paper-backed fusible web (I use Heat*n* Bond Lite.)

Scraps of cardboard or plastic (such as a cereal box or clean yogurt container lid) for templates

*See More Fabric Options ([page 93](#)) for alternate fabric and cutting instructions.

tip

When purchasing fusible web, make sure to buy a lightweight (or "lite") product. The heavier-weight products are not designed to be used with sewing machines and can gum up the needle.

Cutting Instructions

Leaf appliqué fabrics:

For the leaf appliqués, see Making the Appliqués (below).

Neutral solid fabric:

For the block background, cut:

- 6 strips 12½" × width of fabric

  Subcut the strips into 16 total squares 12½" × 12½".

Backing fabric:

- For *each* fabric, trim off the selvage edges and trim to measure 56" long.

  Subcut each fabric into 1 strip 10½" × 56" and 3 strips 6½" × 56".

Binding fabric:

- Cut 6 strips 2½" × width of fabric.

Making the Appliqués

1. With a copy machine or light table, copy the leaf templates (page 94) onto copy paper. Cut out the copied paper shapes and use them to trace the templates onto scraps of cardboard or plastic to make 1 small and 1 large reusable leaf appliqué template.

2. Cut the fusible web into 16 pieces 9" × 9". Follow the manufacturer's directions to iron each piece to the wrong side of a fabric scrap.

3. Use the templates and a pencil to trace 12 large and 12 small petal shapes onto the paper side of each piece of fusible web.

4. Cut out the large and small fabric leaf appliqués along the lines, keeping them organized by print.

tip

The paper backing on fusible web can dull your sewing scissors and rotary cutter blades. Keep a pair of paper-friendly scissors on hand, and switch out the blade in your rotary cutter before cutting paper-backed fusible web. Rotary cutter blades will generally work on paper long after they're too dull for fabric, so hang onto those old blades (be sure to label them) for projects like this.

5. Sort the appliqués into 16 sets, placing 12 large and 12 small leaves in each set. Each set will include 24 total appliqués and will be used to make 1 block. Keep the sets organized in envelopes or plastic baggies until you're ready to fuse them to the background fabric.

Making the Blocks

All seam allowances are ¼", and all seams are pressed open unless otherwise noted.

Marking appliqué placement

You have several options for determining the placement of the appliqués on your blocks. You can try any of the following:

• Use the pattern on page 94 as a placement guide.

• Use the appliqué templates to draw your own guide on a 12½" × 12½" piece of white paper using a black marker.

• Skip the guide entirely and arrange the appliqués on each block as you go. (If you choose this option, skip Fusing and Sewing the Appliqués, Step 1.)

tip

Be sure to leave room for the seam allowance when placing your appliqué pieces on the background block. To avoid catching the appliqué in the seams, keep the pieces at least ⅜" from the edges.

Fusing and sewing the appliqués

1. Lay the appliqué guide on your ironing board and place a 12½" × 12½" background block on top. (You should be able to see the placement guide through the light-colored fabric.)

tip

When working with fusible appliqué, cover the ironing board surface with a piece of scrap fabric, muslin, or a Teflon pressing sheet to protect it from fusible residue.

2. Carefully peel the paper backing off a set of appliqués and arrange them according to the placement guide (or randomly, if you're not using a placement guide).

3. Protect the block with a piece of scrap fabric or muslin and use several quick bursts of steam and very light pressure while pressing the appliqués in place. Remove the muslin, turn the block over, and press from the back.

At this point, the appliqués should be firmly fused in place. If they still seem loose, repeat the last couple of steps again, using more pressure on the iron, until they are secure.

4. Fit your machine with a new needle and adjust its settings for machine appliqué. Depending on the machine, this may mean using a satin stitch, a buttonhole stitch, or a plain old small zigzag stitch. If you've never done machine appliqué before, I recommend trying out a few different stitches until you find one that you like.

tip

In order to promote a harmonious look (and avoid changing your thread a bunch of times), sew all the appliqués using thread that matches the neutral solid background of the blocks.

5. Start in the center of the right edge of an appliqué. Bring the needle down in the right-hand position, just outside the appliqué, and begin stitching, encasing the edge of the appliqué in stitches. Raise the presser foot to pivot the block as necessary. *The needle should always be down before you raise the presser foot or pivot the block.*

6. At each corner, place the needle down (again in the right-hand position) just outside the appliqué. Raise the presser foot, pivot the block, and continue sewing.

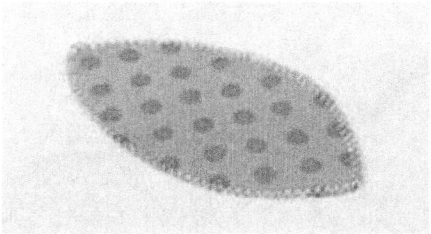

7. When you reach the point where you started, backtrack a few stitches, remove the project from the machine, and use tweezers or a seam ripper to gently pull the loose threads to the back. Trim the threads and move on to the next appliqué.

tip

When pivoting around convex curves and angles (as with all parts of these leaf appliqués), the needle should be down in the right-hand position, just outside the appliqué. If you try out any appliqué shapes with concave curves and angles, remember that the opposite is true. When pivoting around concave curves and angles, the needle should be down in the left-hand position, just inside the appliqué.

Making the Quilt Top

Arrange the blocks in 4 rows of 4, rotating blocks to create a larger starburst pattern at the intersections of the blocks. Sew the blocks in each row together. Then sew the 4 rows together to complete the quilt top.

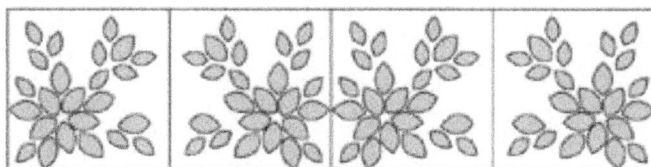

Quilt top assembly diagram

Making the Quilt Back

1. Label 1 backing fabric as A and the other as B.

2. Sew the 6½″ strips together along the long sides, as shown in the quilt back assembly diagram, alternating prints as follows: A, B, A, B, A, B.

3. Sew the 10½" strip of fabric B to the left side of the pieced backing and the 10½" strip of fabric A to the right side.

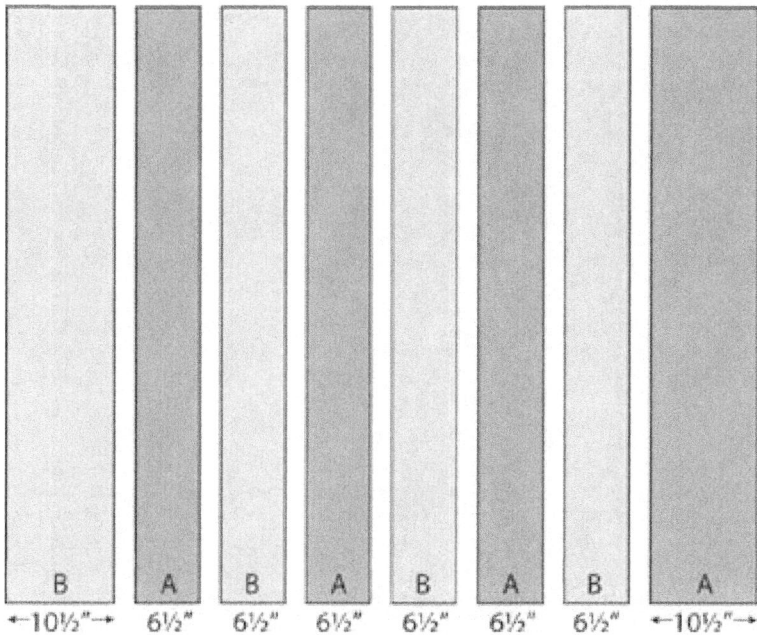

B	A	B	A	B	A	B	A
←10½"→	6½"	6½"	6½"	6½"	6½"	6½"	←10½"→

Quilt back assembly diagram

Finishing the Quilt

Refer to Step-by-Step Quilt Construction (pages 25–44) for details on sandwiching, quilting, and binding your project.

Alternate Ideas

MAKE IT CHARMING

The small size of the appliqués makes this a great project for using 5″ × 5″ charm squares or scraps. To make a quilt this size, you'll need 64 total squares 5″ × 5″. Cut the fusible web into 64 squares 4½″ 4½″ before ironing it onto the wrong side of each fabric square. Use each square to make 3 large and 3 small appliqué leaves and then divide the leaves into 16 sets of 12 large and 12 small leaves. Use these sets to make 16 blocks.

MAKE IT VINTAGE

Appliqués cut from candy-colored vintage bed sheets are striking on a bright white background.

More Fabric Options

Use the following option as a substitute for the print fabrics used for the appliqué leaves:

8 different print fabric scraps approximately 10″ × 18″

- Cut fusible web into 8 pieces 9″ × 17″ and, following the manufacturer's directions, iron each piece to the wrong side of the fabric scraps.

- Use the templates and a pencil to trace 24 large and 24 small petal shapes onto the paper side of the fusible web.

- Cut out the large and small fabric leaf appliqués along the line, keeping them organized by print. Divide the leaves into 16 sets of 12 large and 12 small leaves.

Patterns are available to print from http://tinyurl.com/10750-patterns

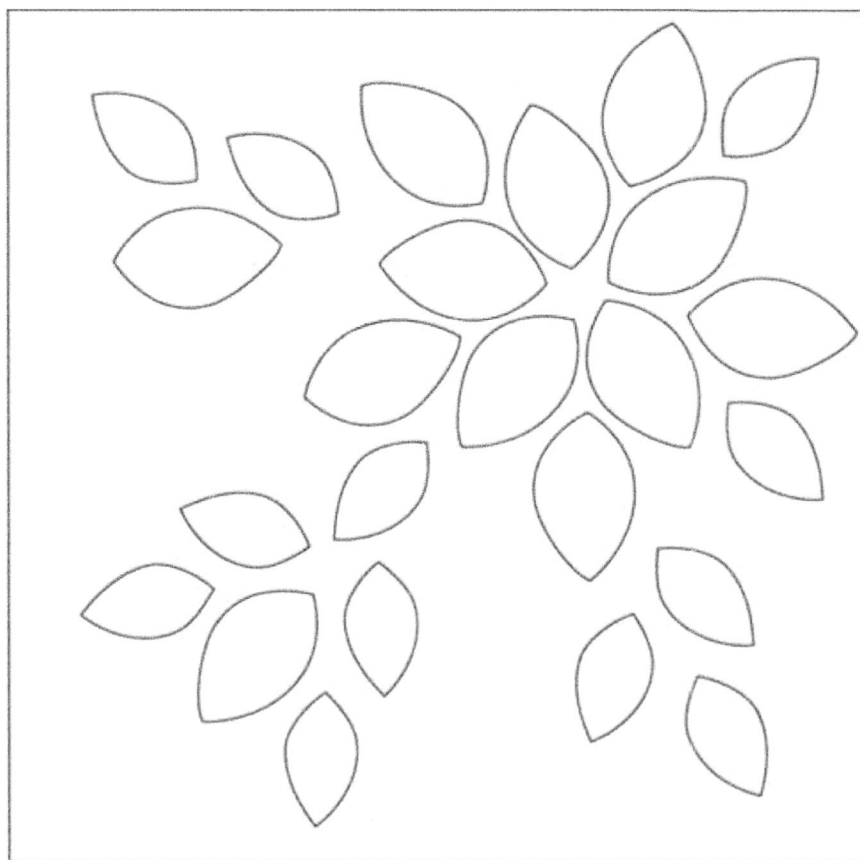

Appliqué placement guide. Enlarge 200%.

Use ruler to measure these inchmarks to verify that printout is correctly sized.

Leaf templates

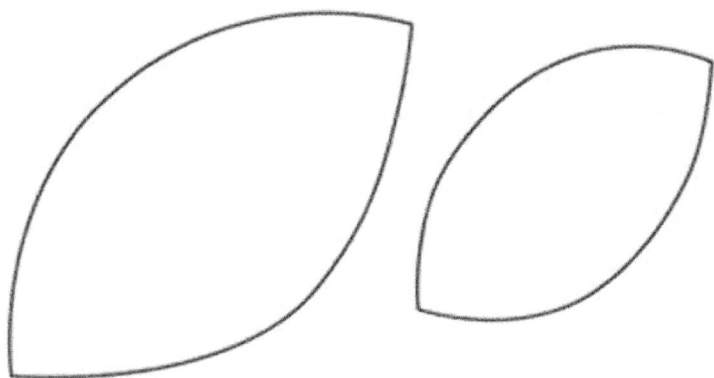

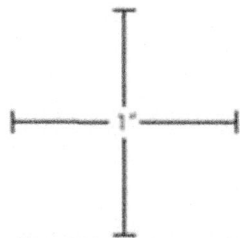

Use ruler to measure
these inchmarks to verify that
printout is correctly sized.

Intermediate-Level
Projects

Superstar by Elizabeth Hartman (see page 104)

Sunspot

Block A

Block B

Finished Block: $12'' \times 15''$

Finished Quilt: $72'' \times 90''$

Made and machine quilted by Elizabeth Hartman.

This quilt is, literally, a twist on the popular "scrappy" Log Cabin block, pairing wonky blocks and sharp edges to striking effect. The piecing of these blocks is fairly straightforward. The twist comes when, after each ring of pieces is added, the block is rotated slightly and squared up, tilting each successive ring of pieces at a different angle.

Quilt back

Materials

Yardages are based on fabric that is at least 40" wide, unless otherwise noted.

⅜ yard *each* of 36 different prints*_ for blocks

½ yard *each* of 6 different coordinating solids**_ for block frames

5 yards neutral solid fabric for sashing

2¾ yards *each* of 1 large-print and 1 smaller-print fabric for backing

¾ yard binding fabric

76" × 94" batting

36 organizer cards

*See More Fabric Options (page 103) for alternate print fabric and cutting instructions.

**See More Fabric Options (page 103) for alternate coordinating solid fabric and cutting instructions.

Cutting Instructions

Print block fabrics:

From *each* of the 36 prints, cut:

• 2 strips 2½" × width of fabric and 1 piece 3" × 5"

From one 2½" strip, cut 4 strips 2½" × 9". Keep the cut strips paired in sets of 2 strips of the same print.

From the second 2½" strip, cut 2 strips 2½" × 12" and 2 strips 2½" × 6". Keep the cut strips paired in sets of 2 strips of the same print and size.

You should now have the following cut from the print fabric for the block construction:

• 36 pieces 3" × 5"

• 72 *pairs* of 2½" × 9" strips

- 36 *pairs* of 2½″ × 12″ strips

- 36 *pairs* of 2½″ × 6″ strips

Coordinating solid fabric:

For the block frames from *each* fabric, cut:

- 8 strips 1½″ × width of fabric

Subcut *each* strip into 3 strips 1½″ × 13″.

Divide the 24 cut strips into 6 sets of 4.

You should now have 36 sets of 4 strips 1½″ × 13″ cut for the block frames.

Neutral solid fabric:

For the sashing, cut:

- 6 strips 13″ × width of fabric

Subcut the strips into a total of 72 short sashing strips 3″ × 13″.

- 6 strips 16″ × width of fabric

Subcut the strips into a total of 72 long sashing strips 3″ × 16″.

Backing fabric:

- Trim off the selvage edges from each fabric.

- Cut the smaller-print fabric into 2 pieces along the folded length, approximately 20″ × 99″ each.

Binding fabric:

- Cut 9 strips 2½″ × width of fabric.

Making the Blocks

All seam allowances are ¼", and all seams are pressed open unless otherwise noted.

You will make A and B blocks—18 of each. They are the same except that they "tilt" in opposite directions.

Sorting the fabric

Divide the cut fabric among the 36 organizer cards. Each card should include the following:

   1 center piece 3" × 5"

   1 *pair* of 2½" × 6" print strips

   2 *pairs* of 2½" × 9" print strips (each pair from a different fabric)

   1 *pair* of 2½" × 12" print strips

   1 set of 4 coordinating solid 1½" × 13" strips

   2 short and 2 long sashing strips

Ideally, each block will include 5 different print fabrics. As you divide the fabric among the organizer cards, keep in mind that the 2½" × 6" strips and 1 pair of 2½" × 9" strips will work together to make the first ring around the center of the block. The 2½" × 12" strips and the other pair of 2½" × 9" strips will make the second ring.

Block A

1. From 1 organizer card, take the center 3" × 5" piece, the pair of 2½" × 6" print strips, and 1 pair of 2½" × 9" print strips.

2. Sew a 2½" × 6" strip to the top (3" side) of the center piece. Trim away excess fabric to make it even with the edges of the center piece.

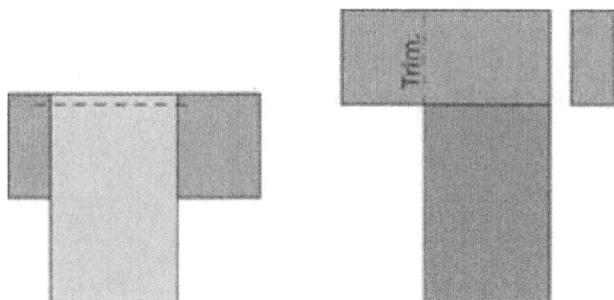

3. Sew a 2½" × 9" strip to the right side of the block and again trim excess fabric to make it even.

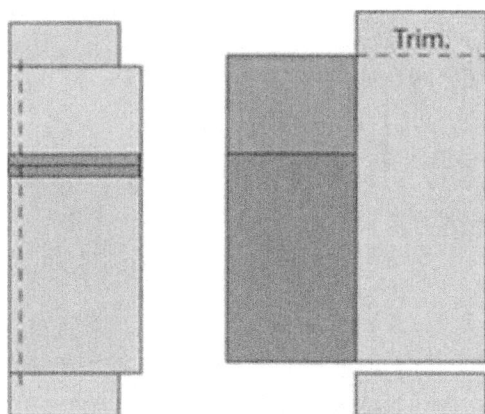

4. Repeat this sewing and trimming method using the other 2½" × 6" strip for the bottom of the block and then the other 2½" × 9" strip for the left side.

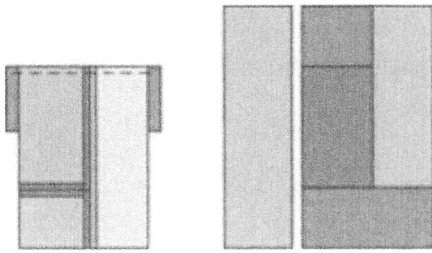

5. Lay the block on your cutting mat and tilt it very slightly up to the *left* (about 3°), so the seams in the block do not line up with the grid on the cutting mat. Trim the block to 6" × 8", making the cuts parallel to the grid lines on the mat. The trimmed block should be perfectly rectangular, but the seams you sewed earlier will no longer be parallel to the sides of the block.

The first time you do this step, it may be tricky, but once you get a feel for how much to tilt the blocks before cutting, it will go much more quickly!

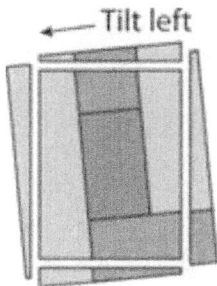

← Tilt left

6. Now, sew the remaining 2½" × 9" and 2½" × 12" strips to the block. Use the same method you used before, sewing a 9" strip to the top of the block, a 12″ strip to the right, the other 9″ strip to the bottom, and the other 12″ strip to the left, and trimming excess fabric after each seam.

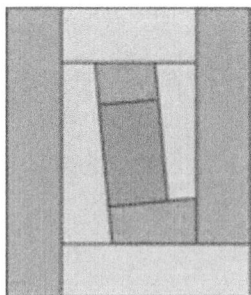

7. Lay the block on the cutting mat and tilt it very slightly up to the *right* (about 3°), so the seams you just sewed do not line up with the grid on the cutting mat. Trim the block to 9″ × 11″, making the cuts parallel to the grid lines on the mat. As before, the block should be perfectly rectangular, but the seams you sewed most recently (to add the second pieced ring) will not be parallel to the edges of the block.

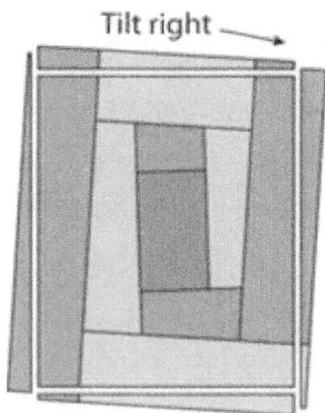

Tilt right

8. Sew a 1½″ × 13″ coordinating solid strip to each side of the block and trim excess length. Measuring from the seam (where it connects to the block), trim the solid strip to 1″ wide.

9. Use the same method you've been using to sew the 3″ neutral solid sashing strips to the block, using short strips for the top and bottom and long strips for each side.

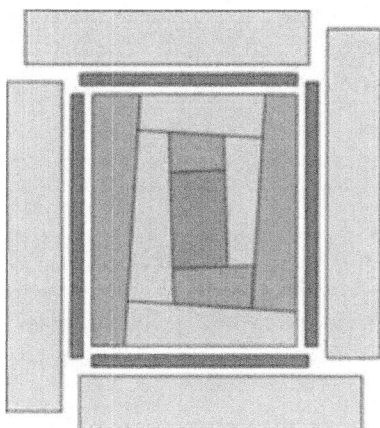

10. Lay the block on the cutting mat and tilt it very slightly up to the left (about 3°), so the seams you just sewed do not line up with the grid on the cutting mat. Trim the finished block to 12½″ × 15½″, making the cuts parallel to the grid lines on the mat. As before, the block should be perfectly rectangular, but the seams you sewed most recently will not be parallel to the edges of the block.

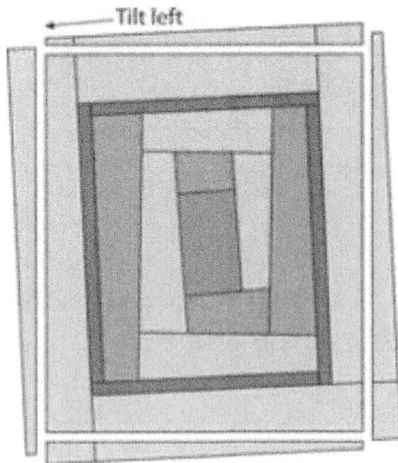

Tilt left

11. Repeat Steps 1–10 to make 17 more for a total of 18 A blocks.

Block B

Make 18 B blocks, using the same instructions as above but tilting the blocks in the opposite direction each of the 3 times they're cut at an angle. The first print fabric ring is tilted right, the second print fabric ring is tilted left, and then the sashing ring is tilted right.

Block B

Block A

Making the Quilt Top

Arrange the 36 blocks in a 6-block × 6-row formation, as shown in the quilt top assembly diagram. Alternate Blocks A and B in a checkerboard pattern. Sew the blocks into 6 rows of 6, and then sew the rows together to complete the quilt top.

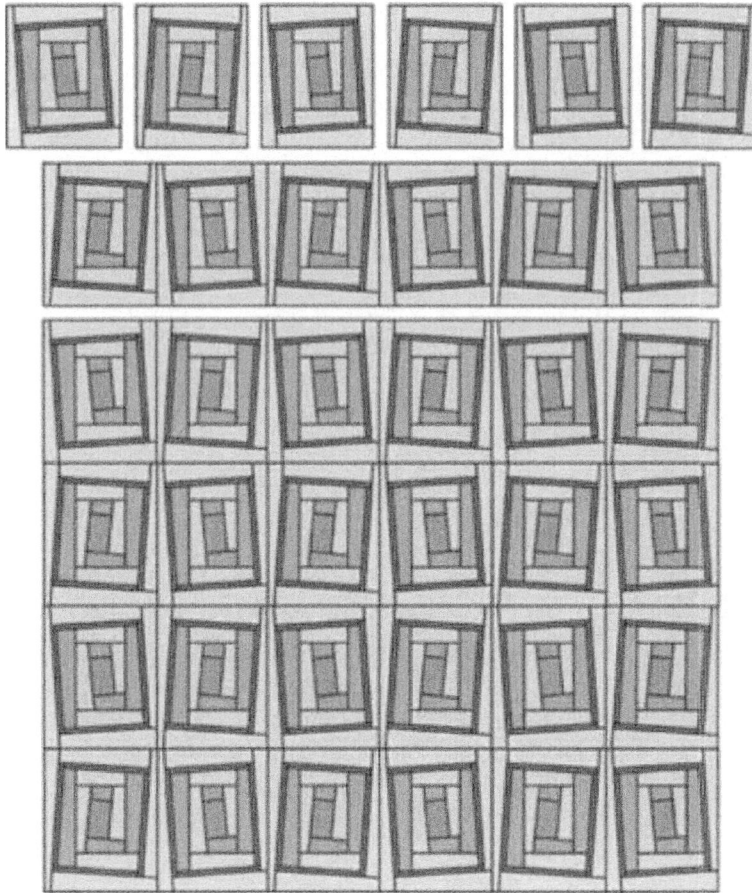

Quilt top assembly diagram

Making the Quilt Back

Sew 1 strip of the smaller-print backing fabric to each long side of the larger-print backing fabric.

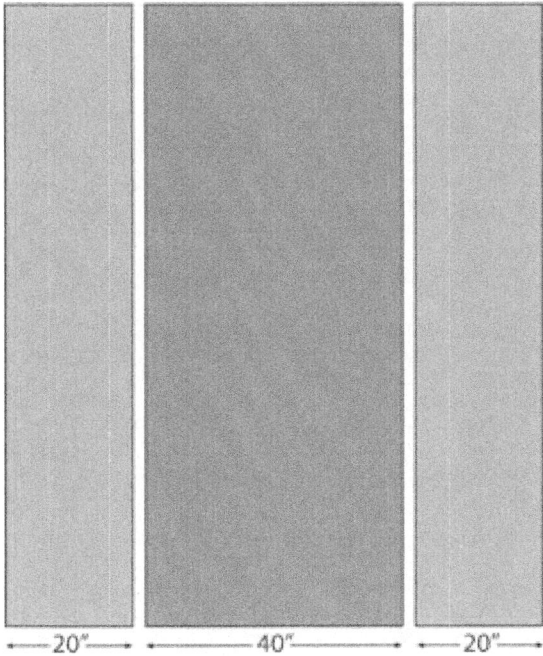

←—20"—→ ←————40"————→ ←—20"—→

Finishing the Quilt

Refer to Step-by-Step Quilt Construction (pages 25–44) for details on sandwiching, quilting, and binding your project.

Alternate Ideas

MAKE IT PLAYFUL

Using crayon colors and geometric prints gives a fun look suitable for a child's bed.

MAKE IT SUBTLE

This more subdued palette would be right at home in a casual living space.

More Fabric Options

For print fabrics

Use any of the following options as a substitute for the print fabrics used in the quilt blocks:

Option 1: Use up your scraps.

For each of the 36 blocks, you will need the following pieces:

  1 center piece 3″ × 5″ (fussy cut, if desired)

  2 strips 2½″ × 6″ coordinating print 1

  2 strips 2½″ × 9″ coordinating print 2

  2 strips 2½″ × 9″ coordinating print 3

  2 strips 2½″ × 12″ coordinating print 4

Option 2: 36 precut 5″ × 5″ squares and 2 rolls precut 2½″ strips each with at least 36 strips

• Cut each 5″ × 5″ square down to 3″ × 5″.

• Cut 36 of the 2½″ strips into 4 pieces 2½″ × 9″. Keep the cut strips paired in sets of 2 strips of the same print.

• Cut the 36 remaining 2½″ strips into 2 pieces 2½″ × 12″ and 2 pieces 2½″ × 6″. Keep the cut strips paired in sets of 2 strips of the same print and size.

Option 3: ½ yard each of 18 different prints

From *each* of the 18 fabrics, cut:

• 4 strips 2½″ × width of fabric

From 2 of these 2½″ strips, cut 4 pieces (8 total) 2½″ × 9″. Keep the cut strips paired in sets of 2 strips of the same print.

From the other 2 strips, cut 2 pieces (4 total) 2½″ × 12″ and 2 pieces (4 total) 2½″ × 6″. Keep the cut strips paired in sets of 2 strips of the same print and size.

• 2 pieces 3″ × 5″

For coordinating solid fabrics

Use the following option as a substitute for the coordinating solid fabrics used for the block frames:

¾ yard *each* of 3 different coordinating colors

From *each* of the fabrics, cut:

• 16 strips 1½″ × width of fabric

  Subcut each strip into 3 pieces 1½″ × 13″.

  Divide the strips into 12 sets of 4 strips.

You should now have the following cut from the coordinating solid fabric for the block frames:

36 sets containing
4 strips (12 each of
3 different fabrics)

Superstar

Block A

Block B

Finished Block: $12'' \times 12''$

Finished Quilt: $96'' \times 96''$

Made and machine quilted by Elizabeth Hartman.

This quilt makes use of several traditional block types. The overall pattern is basically a Sawtooth Star. The center of each star block is made from one Square-in-Square block, and the points of the Sawtooth Stars are made from another traditional block called Flying Geese. The project directions give you a shortcut method of piecing the points on the Flying Geese block using a rectangle and two squares.

Traditional star blocks may seem old-fashioned, but using a more contemporary color scheme and lots of neutral solid fabric brings this one up to date. Each set of two blocks is made from one solid and one print fat quarter, making this pattern especially easy to adjust to different sizes.

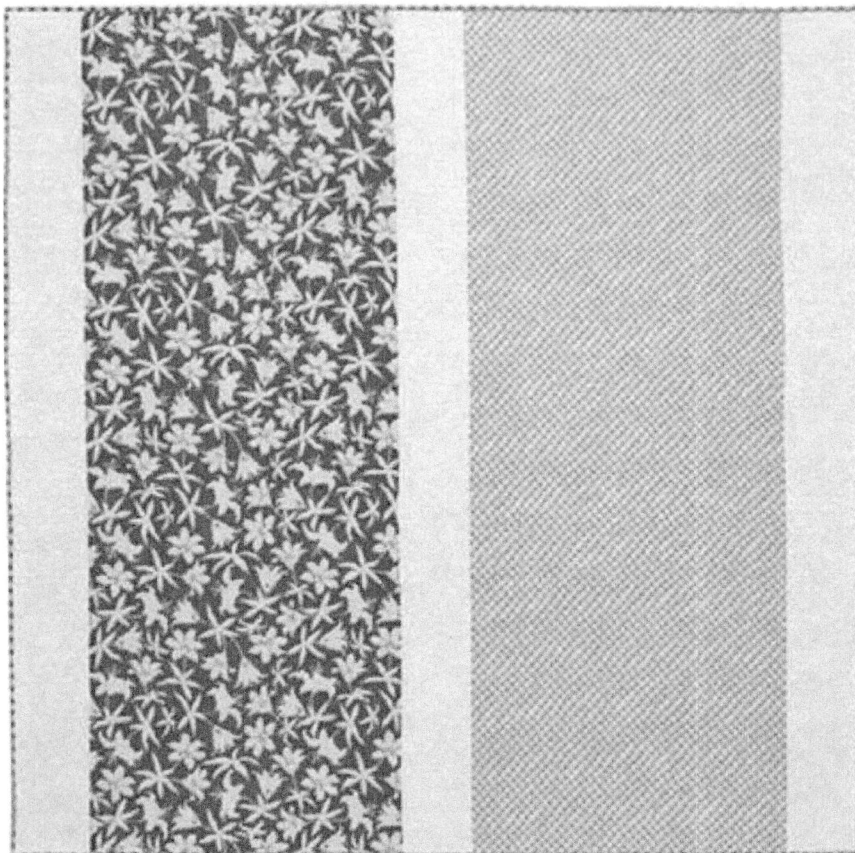

Quilt back

Materials

Yardages are based on fabric that is at least 40" wide, unless otherwise noted.

32 fat quarters (at least 18″ × 21″) of different print fabrics* for blocks

8 yards neutral solid fabric, cut into 32 fat quarters, for blocks

3 yards *each* of 2 print fabrics for backing

3 yards neutral solid fabric for backing

⅞ yard binding fabric

100″ × 100″ batting

64 organizer cards

See More Fabric Options (page 111) for alternate print fabric and cutting instructions.

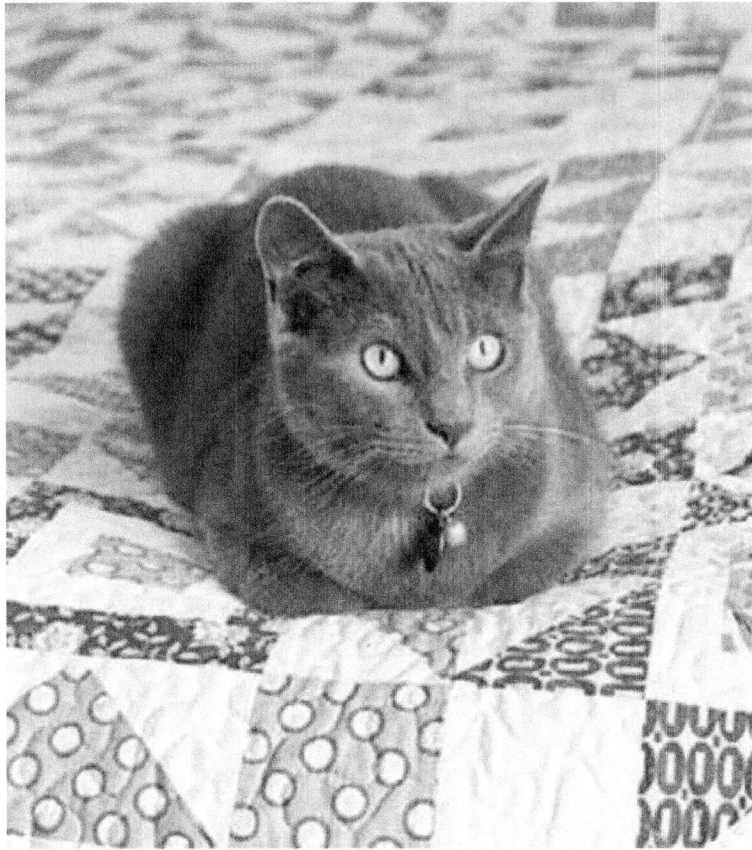

Cutting Instructions

Cutting and organizing the block fabrics

Each of the 32 print fat quarters will be paired with a solid fat quarter to make 2 blocks. Each block will be pieced the same way, but the placement of solid and print fabrics will be different. We'll refer to the 2 styles as A and B blocks. In the A blocks, the points of the stars are made with neutral solid fabric. In the B blocks, the points of the stars are made with print fabrics.

You will cut the pieces from stacked pairs of print and solid fat quarters. As you cut each pair, divide the pieces between 2 organizer cards (1 for the A block and 1 for the B block) as instructed. As you go, place the cards for the A and B blocks in 2 separate stacks. This may seem like an awful lot of fuss, but it really will make it easier to keep track of the 1,600 pieces you'll need to complete this quilt top!

1. Stack 1 print and 1 solid fat quarter on your cutting mat. Align the fabrics so that you cut both fabrics at the same time.

2. From the stacked fat quarters, cut:

- 2 strips 3½″ × the *length* (approximately 21″)

  Subcut *each* of these strips into 5 squares 3½″ × 3½″.

- 2 strips 3½″ × the *length*

  Subcut *each* of these strips into 1 square 3½″ × 3½″, 2 rectangles 3½″ × 6½″, and—*from the print fabric only*—1 square 2½″ × 2½″.

3. Place the following pieces on a Block A organizer card: 8 solid 3½″ squares, 4 print 3½″ squares, 4 print 3½″ × 6½″ rectangles, and 1 print 2½″ square.

4. Place the following pieces on a Block B organizer card: 4 solid 3½″ squares, 8 print 3½″ squares, 4 solid 3½″ × 6½″ rectangles, and 1 print 2½″ square.

5. From the same stacked pair of fat quarters, cut:

- 2 strips 1½″ × the *length*

  Subcut 1 strip into 2 pieces 1½″ × 2½″ and 2 strips 1½″ × 6½″.

  Subcut the other strip into 4 strips 1½″ × 4½″.

231

6. Place the following pieces on the Block A organizer card: 2 solid strips 1½″ × 2½″ and 2 solid strips 1½″ × 4½″.

7. Place the following pieces on the Block B organizer card: 2 solid strips 1½″ × 4½″ and 2 solid strips 1½″ × 6½″.

8. Set aside the remaining 1½″ print strips for now. (These will be used to add a second print fabric to each block, but you'll need to wait until everything is cut before distributing them.)

9. Repeat Steps 1–8 with the other 31 paired print and solid fat quarters. Continue to divide the cut pieces among the organizer cards and keep the cards for the A and B blocks in separate stacks.

ADDING THE ADDITIONAL PRINT STRIPS
Now that you're finished cutting, it's time to distribute the 1½″ print pieces that you set aside in Step 8. You can do this as randomly or meticulously as you like.

1. Place the following print pieces on the organizer cards for each A block: 2 strips 1½″ × 4½″ and 2 strips 1½″ × 6½″.

2. Place the following print pieces on the organizer cards for each B block: 2 strips 1½″ × 2½″ and 2 strips 1½″ × 4½″.

> **tip**
> *Contrast between the two print fabrics in each block will result in a more exciting composition. To create contrast, I distributed the 1½" strips so that almost every block includes both red and blue prints.*

Cutting the backing and binding fabrics

From the backing fabric:

- Trim *each* of the 2 prints and 1 neutral solid backing fabric to measure 104″ long.

- Trim the selvages from the 2 print fabrics and cut *each* to measure 36½″ × 104″.

- Trim the selvages from the neutral solid and cut the fabric into 2 strips 12½″ × 104″ and 1 strip 8½″ × 104″.

From the binding fabric:

- Cut 10 strips 2½″ × width of fabric.

Making the Blocks

All seam allowances are ¼″, and all seams are pressed open unless otherwise noted.

Each large star block is made from smaller units of 2 traditional patterns: Flying Geese and Square-in-Square.

Making the Flying Geese units

For each star block, make 4 identical Flying Geese units.

FOR THE A BLOCKS
The A blocks use the neutral solid fabric for the star points.

1. Place a solid 3½″ square on top of a print 3½″ × 6½″ rectangle, right sides facing, lining up the square with a short end of the rectangle. Use a disappearing-ink marker or tailor's chalk and a ruler to draw a diagonal line between 2 corners of the 3½″ square. Sew along the marked line, trim the seam allowance to ¼″, and press the seam open.

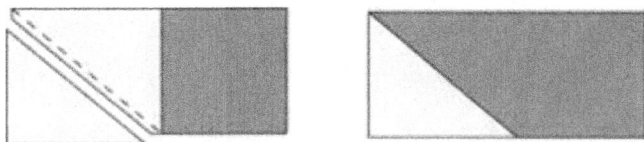

2. Place a second 3½" square on the opposite end of the rectangle and draw another diagonal stitching guide. (This diagonal line should cross the first at the center of the block.) Sew along the marked line, trim the seam allowance to ¼", and press the seam open.

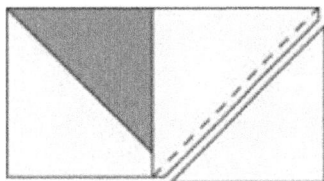

A properly pieced block will have diagonal seams that line up with the top corners and meet ¼" from the bottom center of the block.

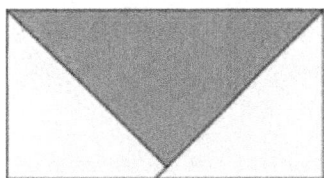

Flying Geese for A blocks

3. Repeat Steps 1 and 2 to make 3 more Flying Geese units for each A block. For each of the 32 A blocks, you will need a total of 4 identical Flying Geese units with neutral solid star points.

FOR THE B BLOCKS

The B blocks use the print fabric for the star points.

Follow the same basic steps as for the A blocks, but use solid rectangles and print squares to make 4 Flying Geese units for each of the 32 B blocks.

Flying Geese for B blocks

tip

If you're comfortable sewing the diagonal seams without marking them first, go for it. I find that my seams are more accurate when I sew along a pre-marked line, but skipping that step can definitely speed up the process.

Making the Square-in-Square units

Make 1 Square-in-Square unit for the center of each of the 32 A blocks and 32 B blocks.

FOR THE A BLOCKS

These blocks have print centers, and the first frame is solid.

1. Sew solid $1\frac{1}{2}'' \times 2\frac{1}{2}''$ pieces to the top and bottom of a $2\frac{1}{2}''$ print square. Then sew a solid $1\frac{1}{2}'' \times 4\frac{1}{2}''$ strip to each side to complete a solid frame around the center square.

2. Sew $1\frac{1}{2}'' \times 4\frac{1}{2}''$ print strips to the top and bottom, and a $1\frac{1}{2}'' \times 6\frac{1}{2}''$ print strip to either side to complete the A block Square-in-Square unit. Make 32

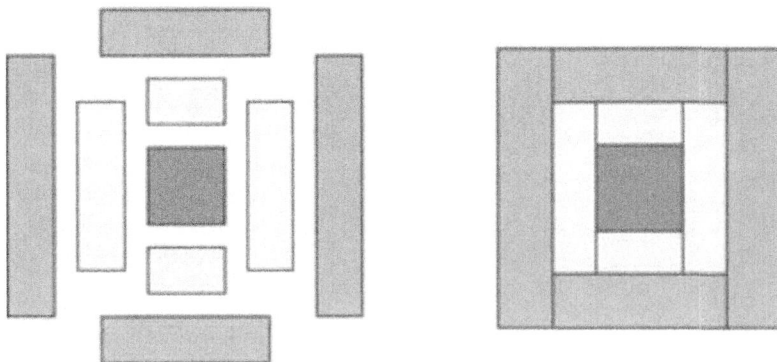

FOR THE B BLOCKS

These blocks have print centers and the first frame is also print fabric.

1. Sew print 1½″ × 2½″ pieces to the top and bottom of a 2½″ print square. Then sew a print 1½″ × 4½″ strip to each side to complete a print frame around the center square.

2. Sew 1½″ × 4½″ solid strips to the top and bottom, and a 1½″ × 6½″ solid strip to either side to complete the B block Square-in-Square unit. Make 32.

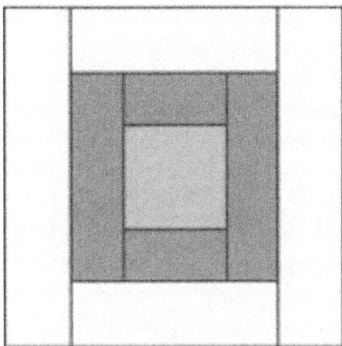

Completing the star blocks

For each A and B block, you should now have 1 Square-in-Square unit, 4 Flying Geese units, and 4 squares 3½″ × 3½″.

1. Referring to the star block assembly diagram below, sew 2 Flying Geese units to the left and right sides of the Square-in-Square unit, making sure the star points face outward from the center.

2. Sew 3½″ squares to the left and right sides of the 2 remaining Flying Geese units, and sew those pieced strips to the top and bottom of the larger block, again making sure the star points face outward from the center.

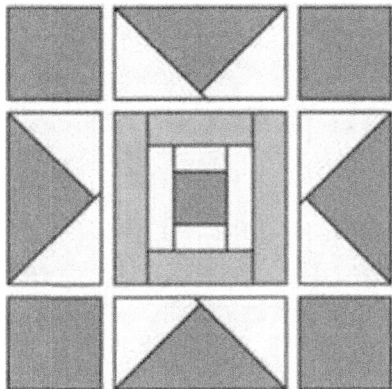

Star block assembly diagram

3. Square up the finished block to 12½″ × 12½″.

A Block

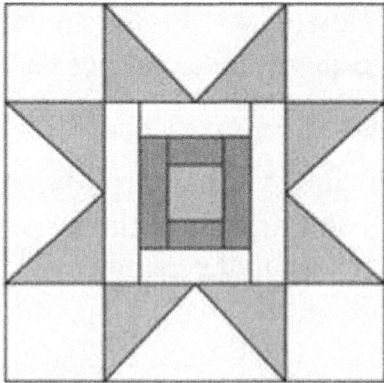

B Block

tip

I mentioned earlier ([page 108](page_108)) that the point where the seams in the Flying Geese units meet should be ¼" from the edge of the block. As you sew the Flying Geese to the block, the ¼" seams should line up perfectly with that point in the center. Similarly, once you've sewn the whole block together, the points of the star will not extend to the very edge of the block. When you sew the finished blocks together, the seams should line up exactly with these points.

Making the Quilt Top

Sew together the blocks in 8 rows of 8 blocks, alternating A and B blocks to create a checkerboard pattern. Sew the 8 rows together to finish the quilt top.

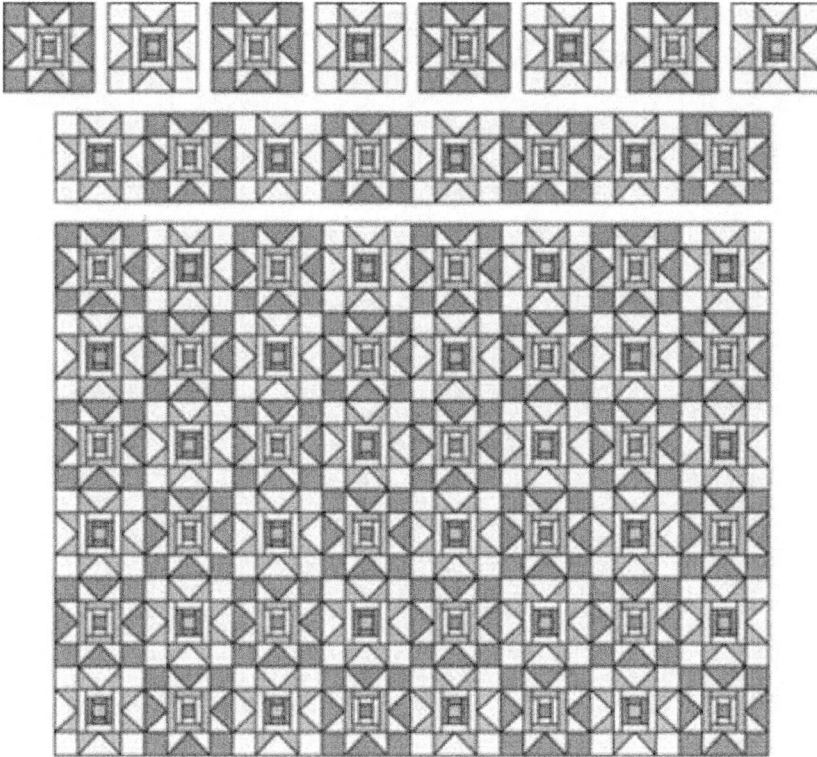

Quilt top assembly diagram

Making the Quilt Back

Sew a 36½″ × 104″ print backing to each side of the 8½″ × 104″ neutral solid and then sew a 12½″ × 104″ backing strip to each print side, as shown in the quilt back assembly diagram.

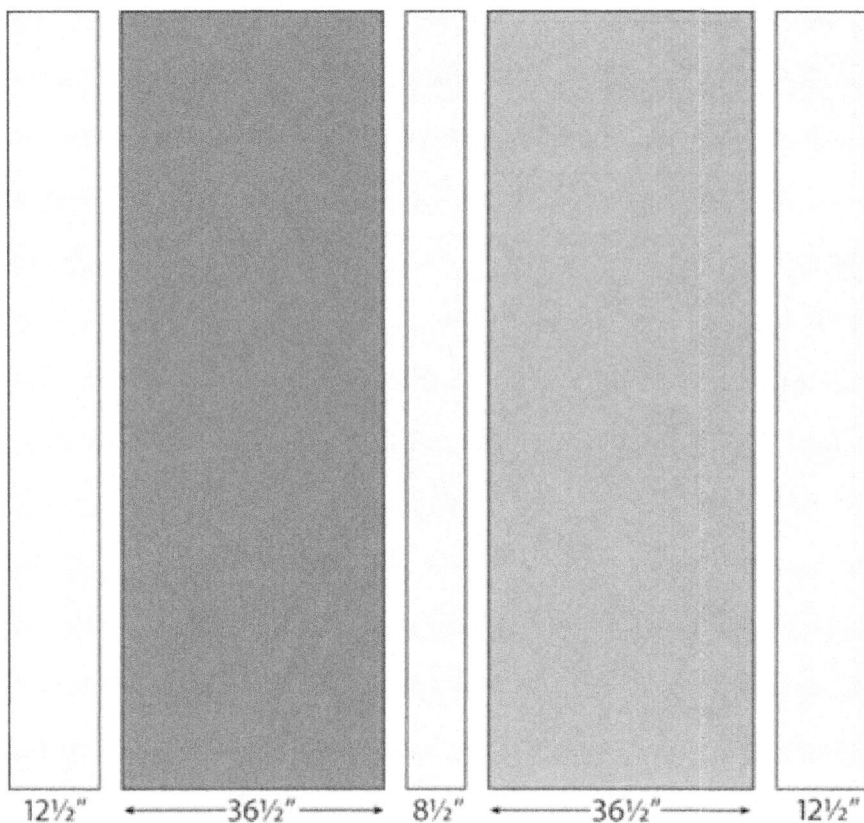

12½" ←——36½"——→ 8½" ←——36½"——→ 12½"

Quilt back assembly diagram

Finishing the Quilt

Refer to Step-by-Step Quilt Construction (pages 25–44) for details on sandwiching, quilting, and binding your project.

Alternate Ideas

The components of the *Superstar* block are so interesting that it can be fun to try a composition made just from them.

MAKE IT WITH JUST THE FLYING GEESE

While the *Superstar* blocks rely on the smaller triangles to create the points of the star, this sample puts the focus on the larger triangle in the center of each Flying Geese unit.

MAKE IT WITH JUST THE SQUARE-IN-SQUARES

In this sample, I played with the same kind of redistribution of pieces that I used in the *Superstar* pattern. I cut pieces for 4 monochromatic blocks, swapping some of the pieces with other blocks to provide contrast.

More Fabric Options

Use either of the following options as a substitute for the print fabrics used in the quilt blocks:

Option 1: ½ yard *each* of 16 different fabrics, each cut into 2 fat quarters

Option 2: 1 yard *each* of 8 different fabrics, each cut into 4 fat quarters

Birdbath

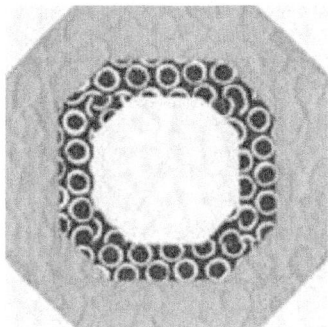

Quilt block

Finished Block: 9" × 9"

Finished Quilt: 49" × 58"

Made and machine quilted by Elizabeth Hartman.

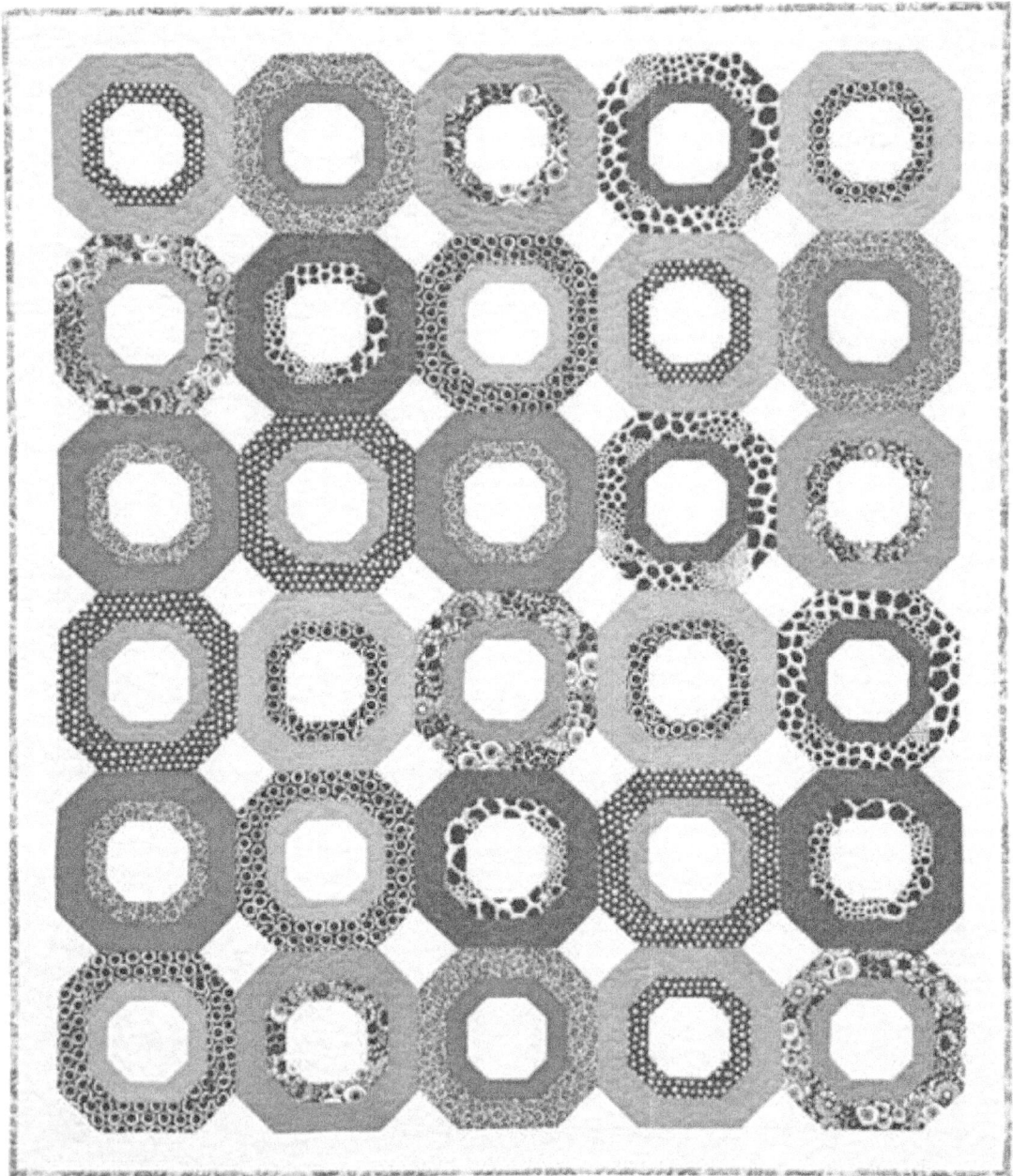

This project starts with the classic Snowball block, which is basically a square with "rounded" corners. The corners are created by placing tiny squares in each corner and sewing diagonally through them, using the same basic technique used to make the Flying Geese in the *Superstar* quilt (page 108).

For this quilt, you build a second, slightly larger Snowball block around the first one, creating concentric rings. Using a neutral solid as both the center and the background of each block creates an interesting loopy, lacy pattern across the finished quilt top.

Quilt back

Materials

Yardages are based on fabric that is at least 40" wide, unless otherwise noted.

⅜ yard *each* of 5 different print and 5 different solid fabrics* (*total 10 different fabrics*) for blocks

2 yards neutral solid fabric for blocks, borders, and quilt back

1⅔ yards print or solid fabric for backing

1⅛ yard second print or solid fabric for backing

½ yard binding fabric

53" × 62" batting

30 organizer cards

*See More Fabric Options (page 117) for alternate block fabric and cutting instructions.

Cutting Instructions

Quilt block print and solid fabrics:
From *each* of the ⅜-yard pieces of fabric, cut:

• 3 strips 2" × width of fabric and
  3 strips 1½" × width of fabric

  Subcut the strips as follows:

- From *each* 2″ strip, cut 4 squares 2″ × 2″, 2 strips 2″ × 6½″, and 2 strips 2″ × 9½″. After cutting each strip, place the set of cut pieces on its own organizer card, keeping the same fabrics together on each card.

- From *each* 1½″ strip, cut 4 squares 1½″ × 1½″, 2 strips 1½″ × 4½″, and 2 strips 1½″ × 6½″. After cutting each strip, place the pieces on an organizer card, pairing the set with a previously placed 2″ set and making sure each card includes 2 different fabrics. Save the leftover fabric from each strip for the next step, below.

- From each of the leftover 1½″ strips, cut 2 pieces 1½″ × 5½″. Set these aside for the quilt back.

Neutral solid fabric:

From the 2 yards of fabric, cut:

- 4 strips 2½″ × *length* of fabric (72″)

Trim 2 strips to measure 2½″ × 45½″ for the top and bottom borders.

Trim 2 strips to measure 2½″ × 58½″ for the side borders.

Save the leftover pieces from the 2½″ strips to use with the next cut.

- 4 strips 2½″ × *length* of fabric. Use these and the leftover strips from the above cut to make 120 corner squares 2½″ × 2½″ for the blocks.

- 2 strips 4½″ × *length* of fabric

Subcut these strips into 30 center squares 4½″ × 4½″ for the blocks.

- 2 strips 1½″ × *length* of fabric.

Trim each strip to 1½″ × 55½″ for the quilt back.

Backing fabrics:

- From the 1⅔ yards of backing fabric, trim the selvage edges and trim the fabric to measure 55½" × 40".

- From the 1⅛ yard of backing fabric, trim the selvage. Then cut 2 strips 18" × 40".

Binding fabric:

- Cut 6 strips 2½" × width of fabric.

Making the Blocks

All seam allowances are ¼", and all seams are pressed open unless otherwise noted.

The 1½" and 2" sets on each organizer card will be used with 1 neutral solid center square and 4 neutral solid corner squares to make a single block. Use the following directions for each:

1. Place a 1½" × 1½" print fabric square in each of the 4 corners of a 4½" × 4½" neutral solid center square, matching the corners and keeping right sides together.

2. Use a ruler and a disappearing-ink marker or tailor's chalk to draw diagonal lines across each 1½" square, creating an octagonal shape.

3. Use the marked lines as a guide to sew the small squares to the larger square. Trim the corners to within ¼" of the seams and square up the block to 4½" × 4½".

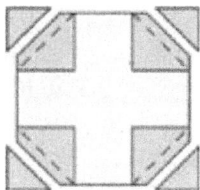

4. Sew 1½″ × 4½″ strips of the same print fabric to the top and bottom of the block. Then sew 1½″ × 6½″ strips to the left and right sides. Square up the block to 6½″ × 6½″.

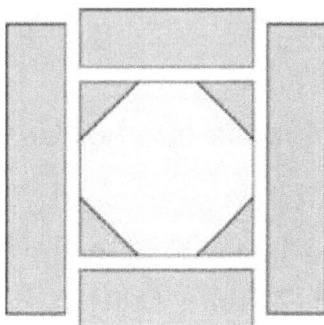

5. Place the 2″ × 2″ squares in each of the 4 corners of the pieced block. Using the same method as in Step 2, mark the stitching lines and sew the squares to the block. Trim the corners and square up the block to 6½″ × 6½″.

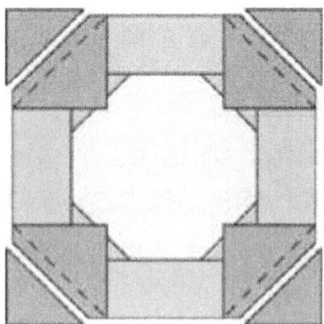

6. Sew 2" × 6½" strips of the same fabric to the top and bottom of the block. Then sew 2" × 9½" strips to the left and right sides. Square up the block to 9½" × 9½".

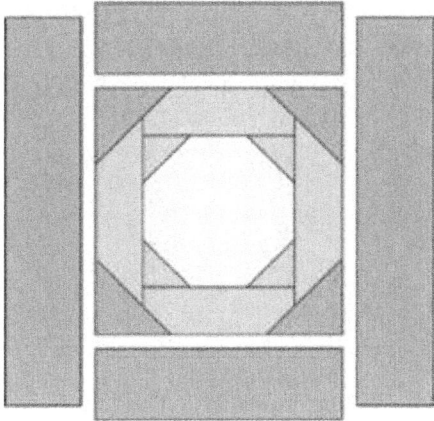

7. Place a 2½" × 2½" neutral solid fabric square in each of the 4 corners of the block. Once again, use the same method to mark stitching lines and sew the squares to the block. Trim the seam allowance to finish the block. Square up the finished blocks to 9½" × 9½".

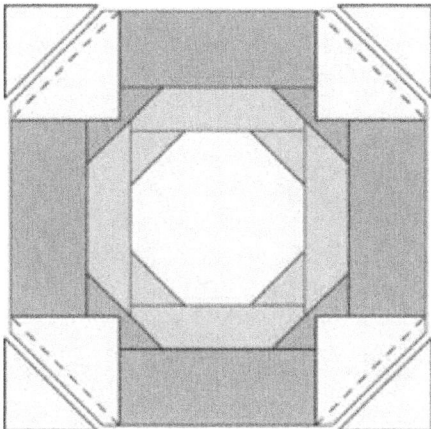

Making the Quilt Top

1. Sew together the blocks in 6 rows of 5 blocks each, and sew the 5 rows together as shown in the quilt top assembly diagram.

2. Sew the 2½" × 45½" border strips to the top and bottom of the quilt top. Sew the 2½" × 58½" border strips to the left and right sides to complete the quilt top.

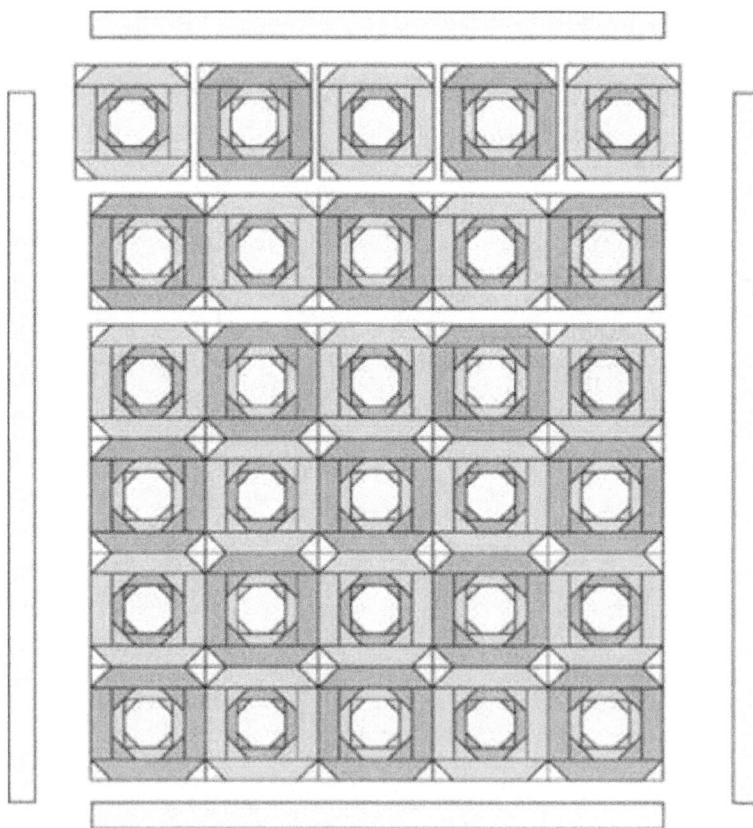

Quilt top assembly diagram

Making the Quilt Back

1. Use the 1½" × 5½" strips you set aside earlier to make a pieced panel 5½" × 55½". (You will have pieces left over.) Sew a 1½" × 55½" neutral solid strip to either side of the panel.

2. Sew the 18" × width of fabric backing pieces together end to end. Trim the pieced strip to 18" × 55½". Sew this to the bottom of the pieced panel.

3. Finish by sewing the main quilt back piece (the larger piece of the other print) to the top of the pieced panel.

Quilt back assembly diagram

tip

If the seam between the pieced backing fabrics will be obvious (for instance, if you're using a bold large-scale print), consider sewing a thin strip of another print or solid between the two pieces. This may seem counter-intuitive, as it will draw the eye to that seam, but that may look better than having a seam where a print doesn't quite match up.

Finishing the Quilt

Refer to Step-by-Step Quilt Construction (pages 25–44) for details on sandwiching, quilting, and binding your project.

254

Alternate Ideas

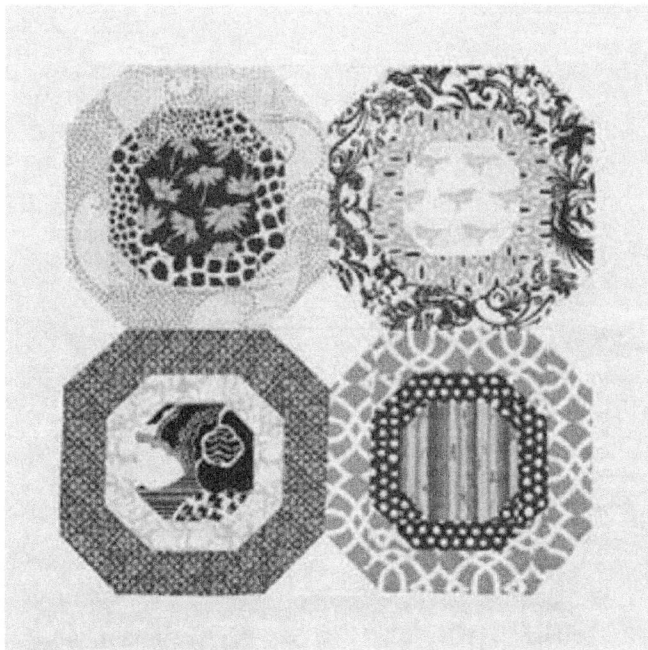

MAKE IT FUSSY

Try substituting the neutral solid square at the center of each block with a square fussy cut from print fabric.

MAKE IT ECLECTIC

Varying the placement of solid and print fabrics among the blocks can make an especially interesting composition. In this sample, I used 2 blocks made according to the pattern, 1 block made with a fussy-cut center square, and 1 block in which I both used a fussy-cut center square and replaced the 1½" print strip with a solid strip.

More Fabric Options

Use any of the following options as a substitute for the print fabrics used in the quilt blocks:

You will need 30 strips 2" × width of fabric and 30 strips 1½" × width of fabric. Once you have all the required strips, subcut the strips as directed in the print and solid block fabric cutting directions (page 114).

Option 1: 30 precut or scrap 1½" strips and 30 precut or scrap 2½" strips

• Trim the 2½" strips down to 2".

Option 2: ¼ yard *each* of 15 different fabrics

From *each* of the fabrics, cut:

• 2 strips 2" × width of fabric and 2 strips 1½" × width of fabric

Option 3: ⅝ yard *each* of 6 different fabrics

From *each* of the fabrics, cut:

• 5 strips 2" × width of fabric and 5 strips 1½" × width of fabric

Rain or Shine

Quilt block

Finished Block: 10″ × 10″

Finished Quilt: 50″ × 62″

Made and machine quilted by Elizabeth Hartman.

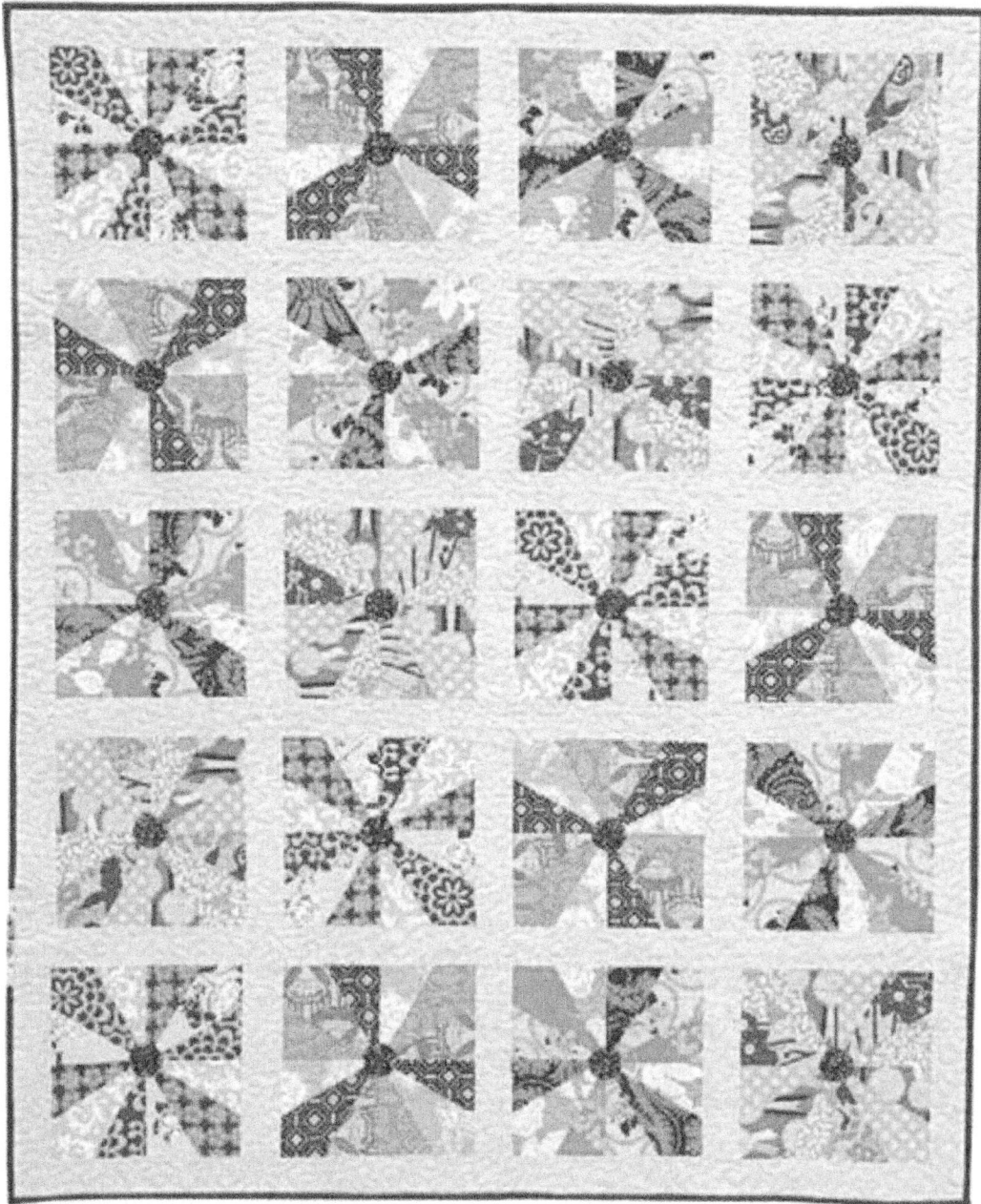

This project is so named because I thought the finished block looked like both a sunburst and the top of an umbrella!

These blocks may look complicated, but they're each made from just four squares that are cut, sorted, and sewn back together again. The method is similar to the technique used to make the quarter-square triangles for the *Planetarium* quilt (page 84), but in this case, the squares are cut into triangles and kite shapes using a 30° angle that's somewhat unusual for patchwork.

Subtle rosettes in the center of each block cover the convergence of multiple seam allowances at each block's center and eliminate the need to quilt over them.

Quilt back

Materials

Yardages are based on fabric that is at least 40" wide, unless otherwise noted.

¼ yard *each* of 16 different print fabrics*, for blocks

½ yard slightly darker or otherwise contrasting print fabric, for rosettes and backing stripe

1⅞ yards neutral solid fabric, for sashing

1¾ yards *each* of 2 print fabrics, for backing

½ yard binding fabric

54" × 66" batting

20 organizer cards

5½" × 5½" square ruler (*optional*)

See More Fabric Options (page 125) for alternate block fabric and cutting instructions.

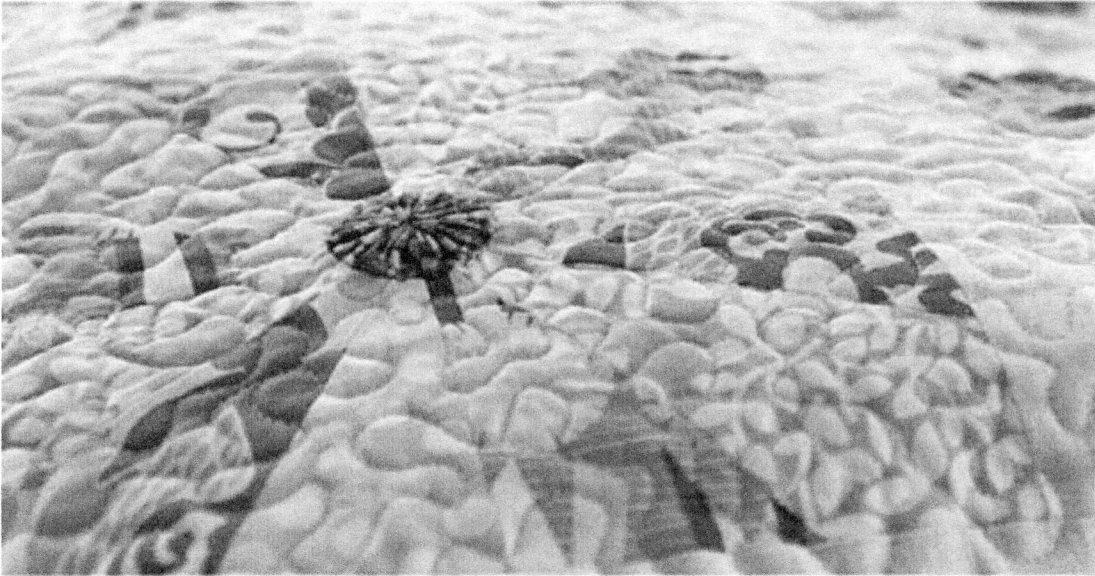

Cutting Instructions

Print block fabrics:

From *each* of the 16 different fabrics, cut:

- 1 strip 6¼" × width of fabric

Subcut the strip into 5 squares 6¼" × 6¼".

Darker contrasting fabric:

- Cut 2 strips 1½" × width of fabric for the backing stripe.
- Save the remaining fabric for making the rosettes (page 123).

Neutral solid fabric:

For the sashing, cut:

- 2 strips 2½" × *length* of fabric for side sashing
- 6 strips 2½" × *length* of fabric

Trim each strip to 2½″ × 46½″ for horizontal sashing pieces.

- 1 strip 10½″ × *length* of fabric

Subcut into 15 vertical sashing pieces, each 2½″ × 10½″.

Backing fabric:

- From *each* of the 2 prints, trim the fabric to measure 35″ × 58″, after removing the selvages.

Binding fabric:

- Cut 6 strips 2½″ × width of fabric.

Making the Blocks

All seam allowances are ¼″, and all seams are pressed open unless otherwise noted.

Cut the angled pieces

1. Divide the 6¼″ squares among the 20 organizer cards, placing 4 squares on each card. The pieces on each card will become 1 block. Mix the fabrics for each block to make interesting combinations.

2. Place 1 square on your cutting mat. Use a disappearing-ink marker or tailor's chalk to make small marks on the bottom and right sides of the square, each measuring 2¾″ from the bottom-right corner as shown below.

3. Use a ruler to create a straight line between the mark on the bottom of the square and the upper-left corner of the block. Cut along the line with the ruler, creating a triangle-shaped piece with a 30° angle (triangle 1).

4. Make another cut between the mark on the right side of the block and the upper-left corner, creating another triangle-shaped piece (triangle 2) and 1 kite-shaped piece, both with 30° angles.

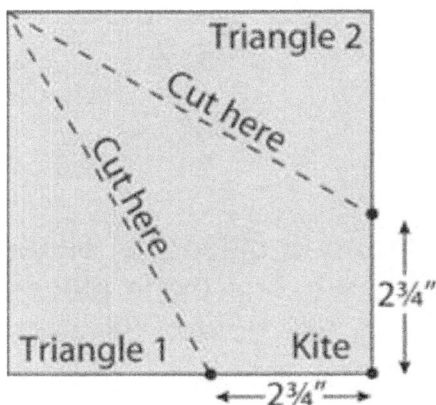

5. Repeat Steps 2–4 with the remaining 6¼" squares and place the cut pieces back on the organizer cards.

tip

Cutting more than one square at once can save time, but be sure to maintain accuracy. (I cut four of my squares, or one block, at a time.)

Join the pieces

1. Lay the pieces from 1 organizer card on your work surface, arranging the 12 pieces so that the 4 prints are placed as shown.

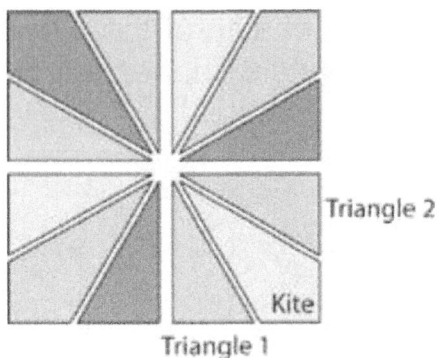
Triangle 2

Kite

Triangle 1

2. Sew 1 kite-shaped piece to the triangle-shaped pieces on either side, creating a block quadrant. It can be tricky to line these pieces up, but a good guideline is to always match the points. Sew the other pieces together to create the other 3 block quadrants.

You'll probably notice that the blocks look kind of wonky. Don't worry!

3. Trim each block quadrant to a perfect 5½" × 5½" square. Measure from the point where the 3 pieces meet, making sure to leave yourself a ¼" seam allowance.

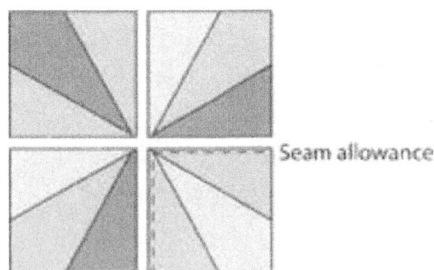
Seam allowance

tip

A 5½" × 5½" square ruler with a diagonal line through its center will make trimming these blocks much easier.

4. Sew 2 block quadrants together to make a block half, matching the corners where points meet. Sew the other 2 block quadrants together to make the second block half. Sew the 2 halves together to complete the block, again matching the corners where points meet.

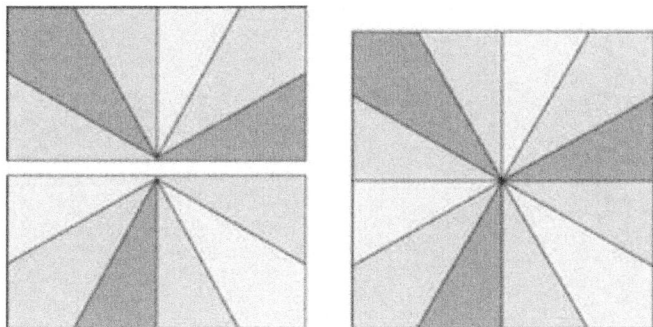

There are a lot of seam allowances coming together in the center of this block. It may take a little more steam and pressure on your iron, but the blocks will look better if you take the time to press all the seams open. Don't worry if the point where the pieces meet in the center of the block isn't exactly right. The rosettes we're adding will help hide any imperfections.

5. Square up the blocks to 10½" × 10½".

Making the Rosettes

These rosettes are circles of fabric that you gather up and sew by hand to the quilt top.

1. Use scrap cardboard or plastic (such as a cereal box or yogurt container lid) to make a circular template 3" in diameter.

2. With a disappearing-ink marker or tailor's chalk, trace 20 circles onto the wrong side of the remaining rosette fabric. Cut out the circles.

3. To make a rosette, turn the edge of the fabric circle toward the wrong side by about ¼". With a needle and thread (anchor the thread with a knot), begin hand sewing around the edge of the fabric circle, continuing to fold the fabric evenly toward the inside and making even stitches about ¼" apart.

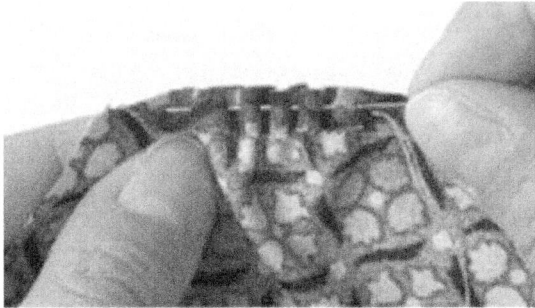

4. When you've sewn all the way around to the point where you started, pull the thread, gathering the fabric and closing up the center. Finger-press the rosette flat, and tie and trim the thread.

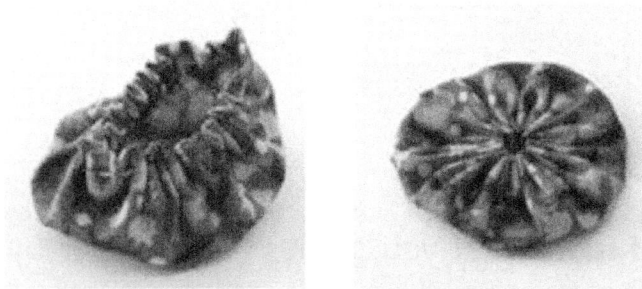

5. Hand stitch a rosette to the center of each block. Refer to the instructions for hand finishing binding (page 43) for hand stitching instructions.

Making the Quilt Top

1. Arrange the blocks in 5 rows of 4 blocks each. Sew each row of blocks together, beginning and ending with a block, and sewing vertical sashing strips between the blocks as shown in the quilt top assembly diagram.

2. Sew together the rows, adding horizontal sashing strips between rows. Sew a horizontal sashing strip to the top and bottom of the quilt top.

3. Finish the quilt top by sewing the longer side sashing pieces to either side. Trim excess length at the corners to make a perfectly rectangular quilt top.

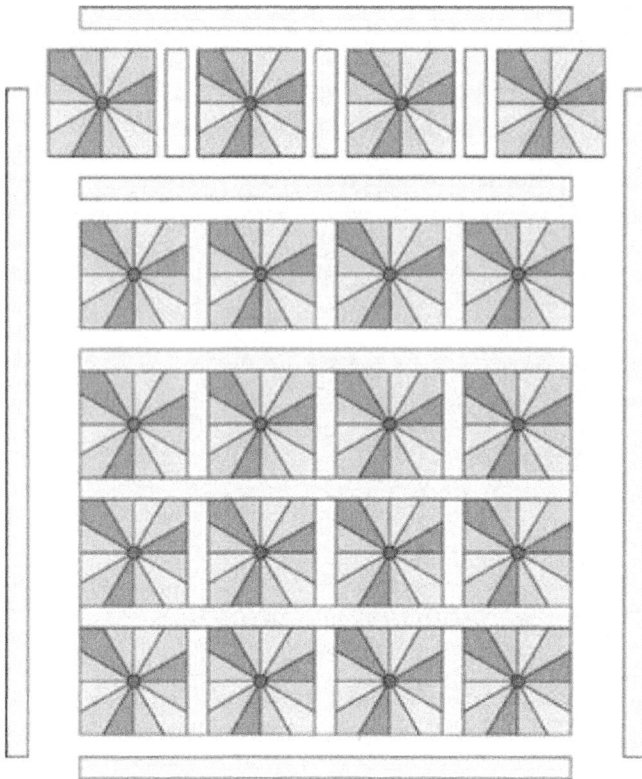

Quilt top assembly diagram

Making the Quilt Back

Join the 1½″ backing strips to make a continuous strip about 80″ long. Trim it to 58″ and sew it between the 2 backing pieces 35″ × 58″, matching long sides.

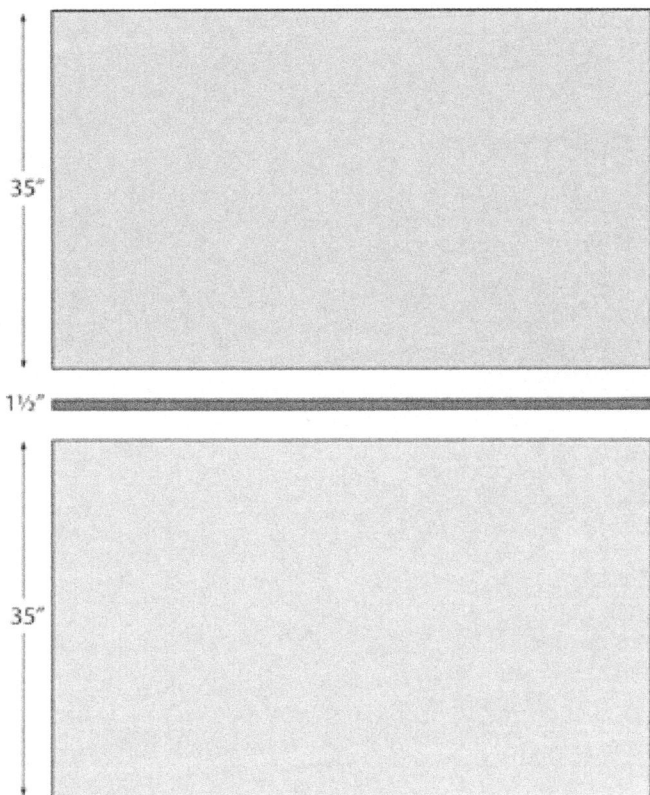

Quilt back assembly diagram

Finishing the Quilt

Refer to Step-by-Step Quilt Construction (pages 25–44) for details on sandwiching, quilting, and binding your project.

Alternate Ideas

MAKE A COLOR WHEEL

The layout of this block is perfect for making a mini color wheel out of fabric. To make a quilt this size, you'll need 7 squares 6¼″ × 6¼″ each of 12 different colors (red, red-orange, orange, orange-yellow, yellow, yellow-green, green, green-blue, blue, blue-violet, violet, and violet-red). Cut the squares as directed in the pattern, using 1 piece of each color in each block. You'll end up with 1 additional block, which you can use for a matching pillow, mini quilt, or other project.

MAKE IT MOD

Switch things up by using all black-and-white prints for the blocks and a brightly colored solid sashing.

More Fabric Options

Use either of the following options as a substitute for the print fabrics used in the quilt blocks:

Option 1: 80 different 6¼" squares cut from scraps

Option 2: ½ yard *each* of 8 different print fabrics

• From each fabric, cut 2 strips 6¼" × width of fabric. Subcut into 10 squares 6¼" × 6¼".

EARLY BIRD BOOKS

C&T PUBLISHING
Another Maker Inspired!

Love this book?

Choose another ebook
on us from a selection of
similar titles!

- or -

Not loving this book?

No worries - choose another
ebook on us from a selection
of alternate titles!

CLAIM YOUR FREE EBOOK

Final Words

A book's completion is a massive undertaking that requires the assistance and contributions of numerous people. As I think back on this experience, I'm incredibly appreciative of all the people who have helped me along the way and made this project a reality.

I want to thank my family first and foremost because they have always been my biggest supporters. Even when the writing process was difficult, their unwavering love and support kept me going.

Throughout the writing process, my friends served as a source of inspiration and encouragement, and I want to express my gratitude for their invaluable contributions. I am sincerely appreciative of how their enthusiasm and criticism helped to mold my ideas and writing.

In addition, I want to say how grateful I am for the life lessons that have shaped my writing. These experiences have given me a distinctive perspective and have assisted me in creating a work that is both honest and authentic, whether through personal struggles or triumphant moments.

I also want to express my sincere gratitude to the many people and organizations that have given me research resources, information, and data. Their assistance has been crucial in assisting me in developing my ideas and producing precise and accurate writing.

Additionally, I want to express my gratitude to the academic and professional networks that have helped me succeed throughout my career. My development as a writer and a person has been greatly aided by their advice and mentoring.

I'm also appreciative of the colleagues and collaborators who helped me hone my concepts and who offered me insightful criticism as I was writing.

Last but not least, I'd like to thank my readers, who inspire me to write. Your interest in my writing and your comments have motivated me to keep writing and aim for excellence in everything I do.

In conclusion, writing a book is a team effort that needs the assistance and input of numerous people. I am appreciative of the support I have received from my family, friends, life experiences, personal knowledge, research, study, colleagues, and readers. I appreciate you joining me on this journey, and I hope that this work will have a meaningful impact on you.

Kirstye .Q Atkinsonb

Printed in Great Britain
by Amazon

26368651R00163